MW00427230

Other Books by Linda Sharon Sanders

The Dream of the Lord, God's Trying to Tell You Something

The Power of the Vow, the Christian's Guide to Negotiating with Almighty God

Prophetic Finance, The Christian's Guide to Creating Wealth with the Spoken Word

How to Pray & Take Dominion Over Dangerous Storms, Tornados and Hurricanes

Points of Redemption, The Blood Drops of Jesus

THE CHRISTIAN'S GUIDE TO BIBLICAL DREAM INTERPRETATION & BIBLICAL SYMBOLISM

Linda Sharon Sanders

The Christian's Guide
to
Biblical Dream Interpretation
and
Biblical Symbolism

ISBN-9781099162282

Copyright © 2019 Linda Sharon Sanders

Jehovah Jireh Publishing

DEDICATION

This book is dedicated to my heavenly Overseers, the Holy Spirit, the Lord Jesus Christ and my Heavenly Father. I love You!

My grandchildren along with the rest of my family, I love you!

.

CONTENTS

Acknowledgment

I would like to acknowledge the Bible is God's final written authority as manifested in the Word of God.

CHAPTER ONE
Why Use the Bible to Interpret a Dream?

2 Timothy 3:16
All scripture is given by inspiration of God, and is profitable for doctrine, for reproof, for correction, for instruction in righteousness:

I think we know what the word *all* means. God inspired every word and divinely breathed on men to write the Bible. The almighty God purposely conveyed words and symbols. He designed their meaning and understanding to be revealed in the Bible. This is the same God who pours out His Spirit upon us and gives us dreams and visions containing these identical elements. Why? So we can discern what He is saying to us apart from the obvious. Everything we need to know about our personal lives and destinies is not written in the Bible. Therefore, God will use a dream.

Why look to man's wisdom, apart from the Holy Spirit alone, when God has provided wisdom for the interpretation of dreams in His word? What does man know in comparison to God? Yes, for a time God used the prophets to give, interpret and present His dreams, but now we have the Word of God written down for us. We can now use His word to determine what these things mean.

Hosea 12:10
I have also spoken by the prophets, and I have multiplied visions, and used similitudes, by the ministry of the prophets.

God used every possible means to speak, instruct and guide His people. His primary method, especially before the ascent of the Holy Spirit, was to send a prophet! Prophets were, and still are, sent by God to exhort, warn and encourage you to return to Him. They, with the anointing, made clear the similitude, symbols and metaphors used to deliver His message through dreams and visions.

We still honor the prophetic voices in our lives according to the will of God but in addition, we have the Holy Spirit directly moving upon us to impart His messages.

Secondly, God has said in His Word that He speaks to us in symbols. Now, this is an act of a sovereign God and He knows what symbols have meaning for you and those that don't. He knows if He shows you a red stop sign, immediately you will think back to your childhood. You will remember when you were hit on your bike at the stop sign on the corner, for example.

Only God knows what has meaning for you and what will get your attention. That same stop sign will communicate a totally different meaning to someone else after their own experiences. Only an all wise, all knowing God could effectively use symbols to communicate to us individually.

The word "similitudes" comes from the Hebrew word, *dawmaw*, and means to think, consider, compare, likeness, or to resemble. When we see symbols in the dream God gives only to us, His expectation is that we will understand the symbols, if not immediately, then eventually. As we seek God by prayer or supplication, He knows we will eventually come to an understanding about what those symbols mean.

On January 26, 2012 I had a visitation from the Holy Spirit through a Dream of the Lord. I had never, ever had a dream like this before. It was truly one of those dreams you receive from the Lord only once or twice in your lifetime. In hindsight, I realize this dream revolved around my destiny and purpose in ministry.

When the dream began, I was clothed with what seemed to be an ankle-length, rainbow colored dress. I was putting a rainbow-colored shoe on my right foot.

When researching the elements of this dream, I found the rainbow is indicative of the covenant we have with God. The first instance of rainbow in the Bible is associated with the Flood and God's promise to man He will never destroy the earth again through flood. Nevertheless, it is a promise, an agreement with man through Noah. Therefore, I sensed the rainbow attire was an indication of my covenant with God. I would even say my attire also was a symbol of my total dedication to God because I was dressed head to toe.

Suddenly the scene changed and I was at what seemed to be an invisible checkpoint. In the dream I knew I was cleared to go through it. It reminded me of the checkpoints you go through at the airport. As sometimes it occurs in dreams, nothing is spoken, but you know. I sensed there were angels there, but did not see them in the dream.

The scene changed and I discovered a tiny box in my hand. I shook the box and some dimes came out. Then I shook it again and a folded five-dollar bill came out. After this, I saw different denominations of bills in a pile, and the top bill seemed to be $90,000.

Right away I can say to me, the dime is symbolic of the tithe. It is the first thing I think of. There is power in giving our tenth to God. In *Malachi 3:10* God promises to bless us abundantly as we tithe. I have been a tither all my life, but I began to take it very seriously in 2014. I made a decision to tithe no matter what and put God first.

I came to understand a folded five dollar bill is multifaceted financial grace. Five is the number of grace and the folded bill represented the many different avenues of grace by which it can manifest. This can manifest as the grace to give and distribute to others.

Again the scene changed and I stood before a road. The road was engulfed by a great, thick, black as midnight, darkness. Beyond that darkness, in the distance was a beautiful display of lights, stars and glory. Just before this beautiful display were two mountains in the shadows on either side. I knew this beautiful display was the Glory of God! It was the revelation glory of God in the distance that really blew me away. I knew exactly what it was!

I remembered saying to myself in the dream, "if I have to go through this (darkness), to get to that (glory), I'm going." I stepped off, and then I woke up. With the presence of the Holy Spirit still on me, I began to weep. I knew I had just been visited by God. Truly this was the Dream of the Lord!

I praised and thanked the Lord so much for the dream. I went immediately to my prayer place and wrote the dream down in my journal. I was still so overwhelmed I only wrote down the major things I saw so I would not forget them. It wasn't until the next morning I remembered many more aspects of the dream and wrote them down as well.

Darkness is never a good omen in a dream. It is usually symbolic of trials and suffering. This was true for Jesus and I knew that it was going to be true for me. The glory of God always follows suffering in the believer's life because we follow Christ's example.

I Peter 1:11

Searching what, or what manner of time the Spirit of Christ which was in them did signify, when it testified beforehand the sufferings of Christ, and the glory that should follow.

It has been seven years since I had this dream and I have come to understand it by and by. I have come to understand preliminarily the symbols in the dream by the Word of God. Therefore, I am certain and confident of what the Lord showed me and I know it will come to pass. There have been many trials, but through the Dream of the Lord, God gave me instruction, prophetic insight and comfort about my future!

CHAPTER TWO
The Dream of the Lord

One of the most important interactions any man or woman can have is a dream from the Lord. Throughout the Bible, even before the dispensation of the Holy Spirit, God was talking to His people through dreams and visions.

The first occurrence of a dream in scripture to man from God is the dream Jacob received as he was exiled away from his home. He had run from his brother Esau who was upset he had stolen his birthright. Jacob was going through a low point in his life. He had made a long day's journey of over forty miles. God bought him to a place where he could get some rest.

He was at Bethel, meaning *place of God* and he falls asleep on a rock. Still in his desolate condition, he had the cold ground for his bed and a stone for his pillow, but God was speaking to him through a dream.

God gives him a dream of ladders reaching heaven. He instructs him to return home and tells him of his future. God even shows and tell him the future of what would become the Nation of Israel.

Genesis 28:11-12

11So he came to a certain place and stayed there all night, because the sun had set. And he took one of the stones of that place and put it at his head and he lay down in that place to sleep.

12Then he dreamed and behold, a ladder was set up on the earth and its top reached to heaven; and there the angels of God were ascending and descending on it.

Jacob dreamed the Lord was standing above the ladder and He declared to him He was the God his fathers. God had communicated this promise concerning Israel to Jacob's forefathers, Abraham and Isaac, and as an heir he was receiving the same promise. The Lord told Jacob He would give him the land on which he laid. God told him his descendents, current Israel, would be as the dust of the earth and all the families of the earth would be blessed through his seed. What a promise!

This dream comforted Jacob in the midst of his hard surroundings. The vision of the angels ascending and descending this ladder allowed him to know God was always at work for us through his angels.

What is the Dream of the Lord?

If you have ever had a visitation from God in a dream, you will never, ever forget it. Twenty years from now you will remember that dream. So what is this incredible phenomenon, called the Dream of the Lord?

The Dream of the Lord is literally a visitation from God, through the presence of the Holy Spirit resting upon you. Sometimes after you have experienced a dream from the Lord upon waking, you'll still feel the presence of God. So where does the Dream of the Lord come from? Consider what the following scripture says:

Joel 2:28
And it shall come to pass afterward, that I will pour out my spirit upon all flesh; and your sons and your daughters shall prophesy, your old men shall dream dreams, your young men shall see visions:

I have had the experience of awaking from sleep and the presence of God was still on me. His presence caused me to weep after having a very powerful dream. You just know the Holy Spirit was there after giving you a dream or vision.

So what are the characteristics of the Dream of the Lord?

Characteristics of the Dream of the Lord

The Dream of the Lord has certain qualities that are different from any other dream. Some of the characteristics of the Dream of the Lord are:

1. It will be unforgettable.

You will remember it for as long as you live, almost as if the dream itself was imprinted on your very soul. These dreams are still as clear to me as if I would have dreamed them yesterday.

2. Always clear, even if you don't understand it.

Clarity and details often accompany the Dream of the Lord. The symbols you will see will be unmistakable. You will not say, "What was that?" A moon will be a moon and a red hat will be a red hat. Your job will be to seek God for the interpretation of the moon in your dream and the red hat within the context of that dream, just as an example.

God will happily give you the answer because He wants you to have understanding. He wants you to have understanding so you can be obedient when the dream manifests in your life. Your obedience will then bring the end result you have prayed for or what God has pre-destined for your life. So then clarity in your dream will bring understanding, then obedience or comfort.

3. It will often follow a deep slumber.

Job 33:15
[One may hear God's voice] in a dream, in a vision of the night, when deep sleep falls on men while slumbering upon the bed,

4. It will eventually come to pass.

Habakkuk 2:3 (CEV)
At the time I have decided, my words will come true. You

can trust what I say about the future. It may take a long time, but keep on waiting-it will happen.

5. It will often have a spiritual or prophetic component.

This dream will have everything to do with God, related to His word, His principles, His counsel, His environment, His things and His ways. The dream of the Lord will often address the future or future events.

6. It will usually seem to delay.

The very strong and urgent nature of a dream can be conducive to the belief your dream will manifest immediately. The Dream of the Lord is so powerful; it can literally make you look over your shoulder and feel that it is about it take place any day.

Well, the straightforward fact is most of the time these dreams take months, years, and sometimes decades to manifest, but the good news is – they will come to pass though they tarry.

7. Subject matter will be speaking to you.

Make no mistake about it; the Dream of the Lord is about you, at least the majority of the time. Yes, there may be other people and situations involved, but ultimately, the dream will speak directly to you.

I had a dream that still troubles me. It relates to a child I have had little inaction with through circumstances over the past few years, but I love.

I dreamed I walked into a house. In the room I entered there was a pool-like structure that actually seemed to be a gigantic sink. The sink started to slowly turn towards me as I stood on the floor. It was full of water.

Out of the water this lifeless child came. The baby was like the fingers on your hand when they have been in water for too long, all shrived up. I caught the child and began to do CPR. The child came back to life and became normal again.

I was very alarmed. I made some phone calls as best I could about the child, but could not determine the child's status. I did all the things in the natural I could do for sake of the child. Through a series of events, God allowed me to see the child was still alive, but the only thing I was able to do was begin to intercede in prayer.

The important fact the dream communicated to me was that I was an instrument for saving their life and revival. God was showing me even though I was not in close contact with the child or the mother, He would use me as an instrument of redemption. One day God will reveal what this was all about.

The Purpose for the Dream of the Lord

Dreams are like little gift boxes with bows on top which come from the Holy Spirit. When you open them to see what's inside, there's usually a message, whether it be clear at the moment or unclear. The truth is God has given you something to think about, pray about and to talk to Him about. More often than not, the Dream of the Lord will revolve around the following purposes:

1. Comfort You

Acts 18:9-10

[9]*Then spake the Lord to Paul in the night by a vision, Be not afraid, but speak, and hold not thy peace:*
[10]*For I am with thee, and no man shall set on thee to hurt thee: for I have much people in this city.*

Perhaps because of a distressing situation the Lord gave the Apostle Paul a dream. He was encouraging him to continue to preach the Gospel despite the danger. He assured him of his protection, as the Lord had people in the City of Corinth. In this way He comforted Paul about any hostility he would have encountered in that city.

Dreams God sends that bring comfort are such a blessing. My mother died five years ago. I took it very hard. I cried every single day it seemed and life seemed so dark. After about a year or so, God gave me a dream.

My mother was sitting in what seemed to be a barber's chair, high and lifted above me in the heavens. She rebuked my unbelief at that time, and she was correct. My faith was very low. She even saw into a healing situation where someone had been sick for many years. From that time forth, my tears dried! I was comforted by the Lord by seeing her in heaven and with the wisdom she gave me.

2. Instruct You

Acts 16:9-10

9 And a vision appeared to Paul in the night; There stood a man of Macedonia, and prayed him, saying, Come over into Macedonia, and help us.

10 And after he had seen the vision, immediately we endeavored to go into Macedonia, assuredly gathering that the Lord had called us for to preach the gospel unto them.

Paul travels quite a bit for the sake of the Gospel. He and Silas, his co-laborer in the Word, go together. However, the Holy Spirit by whatever means does not allow them to go into Asia to preach and establish churches at this time. It has appeared the Lord wanted them to journey westward. Thus, an angel visits Paul in a dream to direct them to travel to Macedonia, as it was the will of the Lord.

3. Reveal Secrets

Genesis 20:3

But God came to Abimelech in a dream by night, and said to him, Behold, thou art but a dead man, for the woman which thou hast taken; for she is a man's wife.

Once again Abraham's fear got in his way. Aware of Sarah's extreme beauty, he feared the people of Gerar would take his wife and he concocted a story to tell them she was his sister. Sarah was his wife, but also his half-sister. It was the worst of misrepresentations because it was partly true. However, when the King of Gerar, no less, saw Sarah he wanted her for himself right away.

Still thinking Sarah was Abraham's sister and planning to be with her, God visited Abimelech in a dream and revealed the truth of the matter. Abimelech was apologetic and sent Abraham and Sarah away with loads of gifts for his indiscretion. God had revealed the truth through the Dream of the Lord.

4. Reveal Jesus

Daniel 7:13-14

[13]*I saw in the night visions, and, behold, one like the Son of man came with the clouds of heaven, and came to the Ancient of days, and they brought him near before him.*

[14]*And there was given him dominion, and glory, and a kingdom, that all people, nations, and languages, should serve him: his dominion is an everlasting dominion, which shall not pass away, and his kingdom that which shall not be destroyed.*

5. Encourage You

Judges 7 13-15

[13]*When Gideon came, behold, a man was relating a dream to his friend. And he said, "Behold, I had a dream; a loaf of barley bread was tumbling into the camp of Midian, and it came to the tent and struck it so that it fell, and turned it upside down so that the tent lay flat."*

[14]*His friend replied, "This is nothing less than the sword of Gideon the son of Joash, a man of Israel; God has given Midian and all the camp into his hand."*

¹⁵When Gideon heard the account of the dream and its interpretation, he bowed in worship. He returned to the camp of Israel and said, "Arise, for the LORD has given the camp of Midian into your hands."

There is no other way to put it, Gideon was a coward. However God chose him to be an instrument to deliver Israel from the Midianites. Israel had sinned, so God allowed the Midianites to rule over them as punishment.

In order to encourage Gideon, God allowed him to hear a dream a man was describing to his friend. In the dream Gideon was victorious. Perhaps God did not give the dream to Gideon because He wanted him to know its message was apart from his thoughts, concerns and fears concerning what He had called him to do, and therefore genuine.

6. Reveal Your Future and Purpose

Genesis 37:8-10 (CEV)

...⁸Then his brothers said to him, "Are you actually going to reign over us? Or are you really going to rule over us?" So they hated him even more for his dreams and for his words.

⁹Now he had still another dream, and related it to his brothers, and said, "Lo, I have had still another dream; and behold, the sun and the moon and eleven stars were bowing down to me."

¹⁰He related it to his father and to his brothers; and his father rebuked him and said to him, "What is this dream that you have had? Shall I and your mother and your

brothers actually come to bow ourselves down before you to the ground?"

Yes, Joseph's dreams started his descent to promotion. These dreams from God gave him an overview of what was to come in his life. In general, he knew he was going to be promoted to leadership one day. Yet God did not reveal all he would experience before that appointed time to come.

7. Activate the gift of dream interpretation

Genesis 40:5-8

[5]And they dreamed a dream both of them, each man his dream in one night, each man according to the interpretation of his dream, the butler and the baker of the king of Egypt, which were bound in the prison.
[6]And Joseph came in unto them in the morning, and looked upon them, and, behold, they were sad.
[7]And he asked Pharaoh's officers that were with him in the ward of his lord's house, saying, wherefore look ye so sadly today?
[8]And they said unto him, We have dreamed a dream, and there is no interpreter of it. And Joseph said unto them, Do not interpretations belong to God? tell me them, I pray you.

God was preparing Joseph for a divinely arranged dream interpretation to the Pharaoh. In order to do this, He gave the butler and the baker who served the Pharaoh at the time, both dreams. Joseph's dreams occurred before he was taken from his home and had to still come to pass.

So God gave him dreams of others around him he would successfully interpret. This would have given him confidence for the predestined appointment that awaited him. Preparation would meet opportunity in a major way as he stood before the Pharaoh of Egypt!

We see the Dream of the Lord is and has been very instrumental down through the ages for God's people. Imagine the turn of events in the lives of the early receivers and all of us if there were no communication from God! I thank God for the Dream of the Lord!

CHAPTER THREE
Dream of the Lord: Abraham Lincoln

God is no respecter of persons when it comes to His dreams. Even as He causes the rain to fall upon all of us, He causes everyone to experience His divine communications, from the lowest to the highest. Abraham Lincoln, was one such man, the President of the United States, who also had this experience.

Abraham Lincoln had two very ominous dreams just days before his death. The writer, Carl Sandberg records one of the dreams which came to President Lincoln one night:

[1]*"About ten days ago," said he [Abraham Lincoln], "I retired very late. I had been up waiting for important dispatches from the front. I could not have been long in bed when I fell into a slumber, for I was very weary. I soon began to dream. There seemed to be a death-like stillness about me. Then I heard subdued sobs, as if a*

number of people were weeping. I thought I left my bed and wandered downstairs. There the silence was broken by the same pitiful sobbing, but the mourners were invisible. I went from room to room; no living person was in sight, but the same mournful sounds of distress met me as I passed along. It was light in all the rooms; every object was familiar to me; but where were all the people who were grieving as if their hearts would break?

I was puzzled and alarmed. What could be the meaning of all this? Determined to find the cause of a state of things so mysterious and so shocking, I kept on until I arrived at the East Room, which I entered. There I met with a sickening surprise. Before me was a catafalque, on which rested a corpse wrapped in funeral vestments. Around it were stationed soldiers who were acting as guard; and there was a throng of people, some gazing mournfully upon the corpse, whose face was covered, others weeping pitifully. I asked "Who is dead in the White House?"

The soldier answered "The President; "he was killed by an assassin!" Then came a loud burst of grief from the crowd, which awoke me from my dream. I slept no more that night; and although it was only a dream, I have been strangely annoyed by it ever since."

[1]"National Geographic reports Lincoln had another dream that seemed to foretell his assassination. On the night before his death, Lincoln supposedly dreamed he was on a mysterious boat or ship. He characterized its purpose

as "sailing toward a dark and indefinite shore. In another version of the dream, Lincoln said he discovered himself aboard "a ship sailing rapidly. That wording sounds a little less disquieting, yet still pretty ominous."

A *ship* is defined by the dictionary as:

1. large boat: a large wind-driven or engine-powered vessel designed to carry passengers or cargo over water, especially across the ocean.

In hindsight relating to this dream of Lincoln's, I believe a ship in his dream indicates a mission, seemingly driven by God. It appears from history, Abraham Lincoln's purpose was to free the slaves, for this is the great accomplishment for which he is known. Aboard this ship he was upon the helm and although they were unseen in the dream, there were many people sacrificed to accomplish this God-given task.

Sailing rapidly would signify urgency and an immediate need for action. Perhaps his innate timing drove him to free the slaves before he was assassinated. This could be a very real possibility for President Lincoln, for we know what happened.

The sea shore to which he approached is more unsettling. Was he headed for the realm of the dead for himself or for the many that died in the country's civil war for the sake of the cause?

Darkness and infinity represent hell and could represent a vast amount of trouble. Perhaps the shore in his dream was a symbol of both. The Bible references the *shore* in conjunction with King Solomon's vast wisdom and understanding, so the *shore* in Lincoln's dream could represent perpetuity.

1Kings 4:29
And God gave Solomon wisdom and understanding exceeding much, and largeness of heart, even as the sand that is on the sea shore.

It has been said it was a lack of protection that caused John Wilkes Booth to successfully assassinate President Lincoln. It seems the President had received constant death threats, especially after the Emancipation Proclamation presented and enacted.

The Proclamation freed the slaves and sent many a southern citizen of the United States into a fury. President Lincoln ignored the cautions of the Secret Service and shunned their advice. God had sent Dreams of the Lord to warn President Lincoln his life was in danger.

One has to wonder how much longer President Lincoln would have lived if he had heeded these dreams. Nevertheless, he still is one of the most highly respected, beloved and adored presidents in our country's history.

[1]Cheetsheet.com/culture/did-abraham-lincoln-dream-of-his assassination.html. Retrieved August 11, 2019.

CHAPTER FOUR
Old Testament Dreams of the Lord

The Dream of the Lord, Nebuchadnezzar

The Bible is notable for describing the dreams poured out on Kings and also to everyday people. Nebuchadnezzar, whose name is mentioned in the Bible at least ninety times, is considered to be the greatest king of the Babylonian Empire. He is the famed king God used to bring the Hebrews into captivity after they repeatedly transgressed against Him. Among the Hebrews in captivity, was God's beloved, Daniel the Prophet. He would use Daniel to interpret Nebuchadnezzar's dreams to bring glory to God. So one day King Nebuchadnezzar had a very unusual dream:

Daniel 2:1-2
[1]In the second year of the reign of Nebuchadnezzar, Nebuchadnezzar had dreams by which his spirit was troubled and agitated and his sleep went from him.

²Then the king commanded to call the magicians, the enchanters or soothsayers, the sorcerers, and the Chaldeans [diviners], to tell the king his dreams. So they came and stood before the king.

This was a potent dream from the Lord. This dream was so troubling the King could not remember it, yet it had invaded his soul. So Nebuchadnezzar called the best psychics of his day. He called the Psychic Hotline, the California Psychics, of course I am being a little sarcastic here, but he called them all to tell them he needed help with a dream.

Daniel 2:3-4
³And the king said to them, I had a dream and my spirit is troubled to know the dream.
⁴Then said the Chaldeans [diviners] to the king in Aramaic [the Syrian language], O king, live forever! Tell your servants the dream, and we will show the interpretation.

Isn't it powerful point the Dream of the Lord can linger with you even if you don't remember it. I personally believe that these enchanters, soothsayers, and astrologers had become accustomed to telling the King exactly what he wanted to hear. I doubt they ever told the King any fresh revelation because that would have to come from the Holy Spirit, whom they did not know. So they gave him information and facts which often replaces revelation.

This group of magicians, enchanters and astrologers probably were very good at giving the King information they believed like his birth sign, his ascendant moon activity, his horoscope, simply put, information that would appease, flatter and even falsehood. It was not any information that really mattered.

Daniel 2:5
The king answered the Chaldeans, The thing is gone from me! And the decree goes forth from me and I say it with all emphasis: if you do not make known to me the dream with its interpretation, you shall be cut in pieces and your houses shall be made a dunghill!

We can see from this passage of scripture, these false prophets came under tremendous pressure to tell their King his dream. The power of this dream was so great; Nebuchadnezzar was willing to murder all of them if they could not tell him his what is was.

Daniel 2:6
But if you show the dream and its interpretation, you shall receive from me gifts and rewards and great honor. So show me the dream and the interpretation of it.

On the other hand, Nebuchadnezzar was willing to abundantly bless the person who could tell and interpret the dream. What an opportunity for God to be glorified! God was setting up the circumstances for His beloved Daniel to be promoted.

Now Nebuchadnezzar was no fool! He didn't get to be King of Babylon by being stupid. I also think it is not a far-fetched statement to think he always sensed they were lying to him. Perhaps Nebuchadnezzar was willing to overlook the overt lying and flattery of the enchanters, magicians and soothsayers occasionally in times past just to get to the truth this one time.

God is over the impossible. But He uses His servants to make the impossible happen. Confronted with the possibility of losing their lives, these false prophets knew and admitted their limitations. This is always where God steps in and creates an opportunity for His people, who were at risk as well.

Daniel 2:12-13
[12]For this cause the king was angry and very furious and commanded that all the wise men of Babylon be destroyed.
[13]So the decree went forth that the wise men were to be killed, and [the officers] sought Daniel and his companions to be slain.

Now through divine providence, God causes Daniel to be sought out. Prior to this however, there is no indication Daniel was used to doing this type of ministry. We have no clues about his past prior to this event at all. The one thing we do know is he knew and served his God.

Daniel was a man of great faith. It took faith to send word to this ferocious king that he would come tell him his dream along with the interpretation. He knew he did not know what the King had dreamed, but he knew Who did know.

Daniel had faith God would tell him the dream. He knew this because he had served Him with all of his heart and had prayed faithfully every day. In other words, Daniel had a relationship with the source of Nebuchadnezzar's dream, Almighty God! So, he prayed with his friends about a revelation from God.

I consider **Matthew 18:19-20** to be a wonderful New Testament promise to those of us who pray:

[19] "Again I say to you, that if two of you agree on earth about anything that they may ask, it shall be done for them by My Father who is in heaven.
[20] "For where two or three have gathered together in My name, I am there in their midst."

The Bible declares God changes not. Daniel, already wise, knew he should pray along with his friends and the dream and interpretation would be revealed. Daniel did not know this particular passage of scripture because it had not been written yet, but he knew one could put a thousand to flight and two could put ten thousand to flight and gain victory over the enemy.

God always uses the power of a group when it comes to believers. That power is multiplied as we come together to pray.

Daniel praised the God of Heaven who answered their prayer with a vision. Daniel could not help but give God glory for revealing something so impossible and something so secret! He saw the same vision Nebuchadnezzar had seen in his sleep and was given the interpretation.

Daniel 2:19-20

[19]Then the secret was revealed to Daniel in a vision of the night, and Daniel blessed the God of heaven.
[20]Daniel answered Blessed be the name of God forever and ever! For wisdom and might are His!

There is nothing like a test or a trial that allows you to access the realms of an all-knowing God. Daniel then went to Arioch, the man the king had designated to destroy the wise men of Babylon. He told him not to destroy them; but to bring him in before the king. He would tell the king his dream and interpretation.

Have you ever been in a place when you know you know, that you know? This is the emotion and confidence that comes from a heart of faith! God had activated a new gifting in Daniel by the demands of a very troubled and furious King Nebuchadnezzar! Daniel revealed to King Nebuchadnezzar what God, the Revealer of Secrets had revealed to him about his dream. How powerful is that!

Daniel 2:27-30

[27]Daniel answered the king, The [mysterious] secret which the king has demanded neither the wise men, enchanters, magicians, nor astrologers can show the king,

[28]But there is a God in heaven Who reveals secrets, and He has made known to King Nebuchadnezzar what it is that shall be in the latter days (at the end of days). Your dream and the visions in your head upon your bed are these:

[29]As for you, O king, as you were lying upon your bed thoughts came into your mind about what should come to pass hereafter, and He Who reveals secrets was making known to you what shall come to pass.

[30]But as for me, this secret is not revealed to me for any wisdom that I have more than anyone else living, but in order that the interpretation may be made known to the king and that you may know the thoughts of your heart and mind.

Notice Daniel was careful to give God all the praise for this revelation. He also reminded the King of those whom he called upon, who could not tell and interpret his dream. Only an anointed man or woman of God could do this. The spirit of revelation demands humility, dependence upon God, but produces the Glory of God! Daniel recounted the dream as recorded in **Daniel 2:31-36.**

God, Who is a God of detail, gave Daniel a play by play of Nebuchadnezzar's dream through a dream He gave Daniel. I am sure Daniel experienced the same vibrancy, clarity and intensity as Nebuchadnezzar's dream.

But that is not enough, the whole point of giving a dream in the first place is to communicate a message, so there must be an interpretation to the dreamer, especially if he is the king of a heathen nation and without an interpreter!

Daniel conveys what the king saw in his dream. Nebuchadnezzar observes a huge statue made of different elements in his dream. This statute's head was made of gold and Daniel tells the king the meaning of this is Nebuchadnezzar's dominion. He followed by telling the king after he had died, another kingdom would rule temporarily because of its weakness. After this, another kingdom would arise that would be stronger and rule the whole world, represented by the bronze in the statue he saw.

Next, the iron in the statue represented a kingdom of iron or strength that would crush and shatter everything in its path. The mixture of iron and clay in the statue in the feet and toes symbolizes a strong and brittle kingdom which will be divided, but crumble as does the mixture of iron and clay do naturally. Daniel continued to interpret the dream by stating God will set up an everlasting, eternal kingdom that will never fail and this kingdom will eventually crush all the kingdoms before it.

God is a Multi-Tasker. With one outstanding and unusual dream He had activated Daniel's dream interpretation gift, promoted him to third in the Babylonian kingdom and caused the King to give God the glory!

But the most important thing about Daniel's interpretation was he foretold of the Messiah's coming kingdom. King Nebuchadnezzar's homage to God and His servant Daniel may have been short-lived, because he soon returned to his own prideful ways.

God would deal with him in such a way that would humble him and cause the King to truly praise God from his heart. God, the Awesome and Mighty God, accomplished so much from one Dream of the Lord!

The Dream of the Lord, Joseph and Pharaoh

The scriptures reveal to us Joseph is a step-brother to the sons born to his father Jacob and two of his other wives, Zilpah and Bilhah. Joseph was born to Jacob and Rachel, the love of Jacob's life. Jacob was 91 years old when Joseph was born. Rachel had passed away and the superior love he had for her was transferred to Joseph.

Now we all know about the sibling rivalry that occurs in families. Whether it's true or not, we have all felt our parents showed favoritism and partiality to our sisters and brothers over us, perhaps. All of us have experienced this emotion. However, in this case it was true. It was something Jacob did not bother to hide from the rest of his sons.

So even before the Dream of the Lord came to Joseph, his brothers had a healthy dose of hate for him. In addition to his constant delivery of exaggerated evil reports to Jacob about his brothers, God was building a scenario, heavy with the elements that would accomplish his purpose for Joseph. Then God gave Joseph a dream.

Genesis 37:5-7
⁵And Joseph dreamed a dream, and he told it his brethren: and they hated him yet the more.
⁶And he said unto them, Hear, I pray you, this dream which I have dreamed:
⁷For, behold, we were binding sheaves in the field, and, lo, my sheaf arose, and also stood upright; and, behold, your sheaves stood round about, and made obeisance to my sheaf.

Joseph's brothers had a good idea what this dream meant and hated him even more for their broadcasted, prophetic, subservient destiny. Then God gave Joseph another dream.

Genesis 37:9
And he dreamed yet another dream, and told it his brethren, and said, Behold, I have dreamed a dream more; and, behold, the sun and the moon and the eleven stars made obeisance to me.

Joseph, in his youth lacked wisdom and shared the dream with his family. Ordinarily there is nothing wrong with sharing a dream with those who are closest, but the dynamic is different here. Two is the number of witness and God had given Joseph two different dreams indicating the same thing. Joseph was excited about his impending promotion. I think it would be safe to say we all would have done the exact same thing birthed from our excitement.

Sometimes it can be down-right dangerous to share such a dream with anyone. Unless you are sharing with someone who truly loves you, this can awaken or deepen the spirits of envy and jealousy within the souls of those around you. When God gives you dreams of grandeur or promotion, it is best to keep them to yourself.

It may be God just incorporates our responses to other's dreams into all of our overall destinies. Joseph's father, Jacob, rebuked him because he knew Joseph's brothers, who being jealous already, would become even angrier. Joseph's brothers responded to his dream just the way that God had set forth and even planned.

Take note: Joseph's brothers were directing aim at his dreams. The scriptures do not say his brothers were angry with Joseph because he was a talebearer, but because of the dreams he had. Eventually God made sure Joseph was far away enough from Jacob, his home and any possible deliverance from his situation. God was faithfully executing his plan for Joseph. He was on his way to a thirteen year absence from his family and all he had ever known. Joseph's dream from the Lord was just the beginning of a divine journey.

One day instead of killing him, Joseph's brothers sold him to a passing caravan of Midianites and told Jacob he had been killed. Upon his captivity with the Midianites, he was sold into Egyptian slavery to Potipher, who was an officer in the Court of Pharaoh. After he was sold, every turn of event would groom Joseph for his eventual destiny.

I can't imagine what Joseph was thinking. He may have had the emotions of Job: I have been obedient to God, why am I in this situation? Joseph probably did not have any understanding about how this bad thing could have happened to a good person like him.

In the scriptures, we never see Joseph complain, criticize or vow revenge against his brothers. Even though we have no information about the character of Joseph prior to his captivity, we can now see the divine working of God in his life. He continued to serve Potipher, as unto the Lord, no matter what.

God was truly with Joseph. This is a picture of God making everything work out for Joseph's good, even his captivity. Potipher knew very well the common denominator between his household blessing and prosperity was his Hebrew servant, Joseph.

But God has plans for an even more intense test and trial. It was after a time of seeing the wisdom of God at Joseph's hand, that Potipher's wife desired him and wanted him to lay with her. Joseph, the man that was truly godly in his heart, refused. Feeling rejection, Potiphar's wife accused Joseph of attempting to lay with her forcibly for revenge. Still, it was a further plan for Joseph's molding and shaping by God.

Potiphar was probably greatly enraged when he thought his trusted servant was flirting with his wife. Without testing the accusation, Potiphar had Joseph thrown in jail immediately. We should remember Joseph had falsely accused his brothers when he used to report back to his father, Jacob about them.

The Bible declares in *Galatians 6:7* "whatever a man soweth, that shall he also reap." This is a universal, spiritual law and it does not matter if you are a believer or a non-believer. It still is God's law of sowing and reaping.

So Joseph is sent off to the keeper of the prison. I believe Joseph may have had a little anxiety at this point in his life, but perhaps he knew God is always in the shadows when we are going through a trial, ever present and guiding our circumstances. He does not know it yet, but his trial is a little closer to a victorious end. God is about to activate a dream interpretation gift in his life.

Two officers of the King of Egypt, had offended him in some way and were put into the same prison as Joseph. Again, this was no coincidence; the plot from the Lord was thickening. Not only were these two officers in the same prison as Joseph, they were under his care to be served. One night they both had dreams from the Lord.

When Joseph came in to serve them one morning, they were sad. Joseph inquired about the reason for their sadness and they told him they had dreams, but there was no one to interpret them. Then Joseph told them dream interpretations belong to God and he would interpret them.

Genesis 40:8
And they said unto him, We have dreamed a dream, and there is no interpreter of it. And Joseph said unto them, Do not interpretations belong to God? tell me them, I pray you.

Demands for interpretation of dreams and visions plus faith always equals activation for the person who would dare believe God. Joseph heard and interpreted the butler and baker's dreams. The baker was hanged, but the chief butler was restored to his service to Pharaoh (**Genesis 40:9-13**).

Joseph asked the butler to remember his service to him, up to and including his ability to interpret his dream when he was troubled. He went on to tell the butler he had not done anything to be in the prison and even he was unworthily sold into slavery. Joseph was doing what many of us do when we are going through a trial. We are trying to end the pain, the suffering or the hardship through our own efforts. But Pharaoh's butler returned to his place, he forgot.

The Word of God affirms God will never give His glory to another. In other words, He is the One that will deliver us and He knows just how He is going to do it. He gets the credit, all of it! The butler and baker were but instruments in the hand of God for Joseph. They were close to and had the ear of Pharaoh. One of them was the very link to the change Joseph desired, and fervently prayed about.

But often when we believe we are on the verge of deliverance and answered prayer, sometimes there comes a delay. This is what happened to Joseph. The Bible declares it was two more years before anything would change. Two years before Pharaoh would have his life-changing dream.

Genesis 41:1-7

[1]*When two full years had passed, Pharaoh had a dream: He was standing by the Nile,*
[2]*when out of the river there came up seven cows, sleek and fat, and they grazed among the reeds.*
[3]*After them, seven other cows, ugly and gaunt, came up out of the Nile and stood beside those on the riverbank.*
[4]*And the cows that were ugly and gaunt ate up the seven sleek, fat cows. Then Pharaoh woke up.*
[5]*He fell asleep again and had a second dream: Seven heads of grain, healthy and good, were growing on a single stalk.*
[6]*After them, seven other heads of grain sprouted—thin and scorched by the east wind.*

[7]The thin heads of grain swallowed up the seven healthy, full heads. Then Pharaoh woke up; it had been a dream.

God engineered Joseph's promotion by giving Pharaoh these two dreams. Oh, what an opportunity for Joseph! Why did it take two more years before God would give Pharaoh these dreams? I don't think anyone knows. But what I do know is these dreams arrived exactly when Joseph was ripe for a great promotion. These dreams arrived when God knew Pharaoh would see the Glory of God!

Pharaoh, is greatly troubled by the two dreams he received overnight. He calls for all the magicians and all the wise men. It is then the butler, formerly helped by Joseph through his accurate dream interpretation, remembers him. He recounts to the great Pharaoh his experience with the Hebrew servant.

You could say Pharaoh hastily and hurriedly had Joseph brought from the dungeon. Before his court appearance, Joseph was allowed to shave and change his clothes. It reminds me of the beggar by the wayside who threw away his beggar's clothes when he heard Jesus was passing by. He knew, like Joseph that all things had become new. Joseph knew this was it!

This was a day he had waited for thirteen years! He had been first taken away by the Midianite caravan when he was the tender age of seventeen. Now he is thirty years old, mature and forever loyal to the God of heaven. So then Joseph enters the court of Pharaoh. Pharaoh tells the dream to Joseph for him to interpret.

Genesis 41:25-28

25Then Joseph said to Pharaoh, The [two] dreams are one; God has shown Pharaoh what He is about to do.
26The seven good cows are seven years, and the seven good ears [of grain] are seven years; the [two] dreams are one [in their meaning].
27And the seven thin and ill favored cows that came up after them are seven years, and also the seven empty ears [of grain], blighted and shriveled by the east wind; they are seven years of hunger and famine.
28This is the message just as I have told Pharaoh: God has shown Pharaoh what He is about to do.

Not only does Joseph give God the Glory for the interpretation he gives, but he informs Pharaoh of the prophetic nature of the dreams. Joseph's interpretation continues:

Genesis 41:29-32

29Behold, there come seven years of great plenty throughout all the land of Egypt:
30And there shall arise after them seven years of famine; and all the plenty shall be forgotten in the land of Egypt; and the famine shall consume the land;
31And the plenty shall not be known in the land by reason of that famine following; for it shall be very grievous.
32And for that the dream was doubled unto Pharaoh twice; it is because the thing is established by God, and

God will shortly bring it to pass.

God uses Joseph to interpret Pharaoh's dream, but now the gift of the Word of Wisdom is activated to show Pharaoh what to do in response to the prophetic revelation of his dream.

Genesis 41:33-36
33Now therefore let Pharaoh look out a man discreet and wise, and set him over the land of Egypt.

34Let Pharaoh do this, and let him appoint officers over the land, and take up the fifth part of the land of Egypt in the seven plenteous years.

35And let them gather all the food of those good years that come, and lay up corn under the hand of Pharaoh, and let them keep food in the cities.

36And that food shall be for store to the land against the seven years of famine, which shall be in the land of Egypt; that the land perish not through the famine.

The Bible asserts promotion comes from the Lord. Pharaoh is impressed and overwhelmed with the supernatural gifting of Joseph and determines to promote him to third in authority over all of Egypt. Pharaoh comes one step closer to knowing the God of Heaven, because he has seen and acknowledged the Almighty God before all of Egypt. Through all of these events, God had shown Himself strong through the Dreams of the Lord to both Joseph and the Pharaoh of Egypt. Joseph's own dreams have now come to pass.

Daniel Dreams of the Coming Apocalypse

Daniel, the beloved of God, had yet one more dream. The Dream of the Lord reveals the rising of four evil kings and nations, the betrayal and deliverance of Israel, the suffering and trials of the saints of God; and the eventual establishment of the Kingdom of God.

Daniel's 7th Chapter records his apocalyptic vision. It depicts the major world empires and events from Daniel's time until the second coming of Jesus Christ. In many ways, the dream Daniel interpreted for King Nebuchadnezzar and his vision were prophetically the same. He interpreted the king's vision almost 50 years prior, but they both uncover what is to come. I don't want to reinvent the wheel, so I will quote what an expert on these dreams reveal.

[1]The Chaldean Empire

"In *Daniel 7:3-4,* Daniel records, "And four great beasts came up from the sea, each different from the other. The first was like a lion, and had eagle's wings. I watched till its wings were plucked off; and it was lifted up from the earth and made to stand on two feet like a man, and a man's heart was given to it.

In verse 17 we are told, "Those great beasts, which are four, are four kings which arise out of the earth." The lion was symbolic of the kingdom of Babylon and the "man's heart" was that of its most notable king, Nebuchadnezzar, who is written about considerably in the first four chapters of Daniel.

As *The Expositor's Bible Commentary* explains, "The lion symbol was characteristic of Babylon, especially in Nebuchadnezzar's time, when the Ishtar Gate entrance was adorned on either side with a long procession of yellow lions on blue-glazed brick, fashioned in high relief" (1985, Vol. 7, pp. 85-86). The eagle's wings plucked off the lion were symbolic of Nebuchadnezzar's time of insanity when he was humbled by God to learn that "the Most High rules in the kingdom of men" (*Daniel 4:17, 34-37*).

Nebuchadnezzar ruled from Babylon to Asia Minor and from the Caspian Sea to Egypt. Biblically, his most notable conquest was that of the nation of Judah, with Daniel being the most famous captive from that nation. Following his father's death, Nebuchadnezzar reigned as king of Babylon for 43 years, from 604-561 B.C. (JewishEncyclopedia.com/Nebuchadnezzar). After his death, Babylon continued as a strong empire until 539 B.C., when it was conquered by the second rising power in Daniel's vision, the Medo-Persian Empire."

[1]The Medo-Persian Empire

"Daniel 7:5 says, "And suddenly another beast, a second, like a bear. It was raised up on one side, and had three ribs in its mouth between its teeth. And they said thus to it: 'Arise, devour much flesh!'"

This beast's being "raised up on one side" represents the Persians being greater than the Medes in this federated empire. This is made plain to Daniel in a vision two years later when he sees a ram with two horns, one being higher than the other. Daniel is told by the angel Gabriel that the ram represents the kings of Media and Persia (*Daniel 8:3, 20*).

The three ribs that are devoured represent three empires conquered by Persia's first great king, Cyrus the Great, and his son, Cambyses II. Cyrus came to power in 558 B.C. and conquered the Lydian Empire (Asia Minor) in 546 and the Chaldean Empire (Babylon) in 539; and Cambyses conquered Egypt in 525 (ibid. p. 86).

The Medo-Persian Empire lasted for 200 years and, under later kings, expanded to Greece in the west and to India in the east. At one point, the Persian Empire covered parts of three continents: Asia, Africa and Europe. But, like the Chaldean Empire, the Persian Empire finally came to an end. A new beast was rising in the west, and its appointed time had come."

[1]The Greek Empire

"*Daniel 7:6* says, "After this I looked, and there was another, like a leopard, which had on its back four wings of a bird. The beast also had four heads, and dominion was given to it.""

As with the second beast, the third beast is clearly identified by the angel Gabriel. It was Greece, and the "first king" was Alexander the Great. After his untimely death in 323 B.C., his empire was divided into four smaller kingdoms (*Daniel 8:21-22*).

The symbol of the leopard with four wings portrays the swiftness of Alexander's sudden rise and conquest of the Persian Empire from 334-331 B.C. After his death, several years of struggle ensued that resulted in the division of his empire into four kingdoms. The new kingdoms were (1) Greece and Macedon, (2) Thrace and Asia Minor, (3) Middle East-Asia and (4) Egypt-Palestine.

"After this I saw in the night visions, and behold, a fourth beast, dreadful and terrible, exceedingly strong. It had huge iron teeth; it was devouring, breaking in pieces, and trampling the residue with its feet. It was different from all the beasts that were before it, and it had ten horns. "The last two were ruled by Seleucus, who began the Seleucid Empire, and Ptolemy, who began the Ptolemaic Empire. These two kingdoms are called the king of North and the king of the South in *Daniel 11*. Approximately two centuries later, the fourth beast conquered all four of these kingdoms and expanded far beyond the lands conquered by the previous beasts. These two kingdoms, called the king of North and the king of the South and having yet to be determined configurations, will revive and play major roles in end-time prophecies."

[1]The Roman Empire

"Next in *Daniel 7:7* we read, "After this I saw in the night visions, and behold, a fourth beast, dreadful and terrible, exceedingly strong. It had huge iron teeth; it was devouring, breaking in pieces, and trampling the residue with its feet. It was different from all the beasts that were before it, and it had ten horns."

The devouring teeth of iron and the trampling feet correspond with Nebuchadnezzar's vision of the fourth kingdom being strong as iron, breaking in pieces and crushing all others (*Daniel 2:40-41*). When the Roman Empire came to power under the Caesars (44 B.C.) it devoured, broke in pieces and trampled the residue of its enemies with its feet—as was described in Daniel's vision in *Daniel 7*.

The fourth beast is quite different from the previous beasts, in that it has 10 horns. *Daniel 7:24* says, "The ten horns are ten kings who shall arise from this kingdom." Historically, these revivals began to rise after the fall of Rome in A.D. 476, with the later ones under a new name: the Holy Roman Empire.

This fourth beast would continue to be revived off and on for over 1,500 years until the end-time 10th revival. The 10th and final revival will be destroyed by Jesus Christ at His second coming (*Daniel 7:26-27*). This leads to one other unusual feature of the prophecy of the fourth beast."

[1]The Little Horn

Daniel 7:8 says, "I was considering the horns, and there was another horn, a little one, coming up among them, before whom three of the first horns were plucked out by the roots. And there, in this horn, were eyes like the eyes of a man, and a mouth speaking pompous words."

This little horn represents a powerful religious system that would align with the last seven of the 10 political horns that were to arise after the fall of Rome. This coordination between church and state produced what ultimately became known as the Holy Roman Empire.

In verses 21-22 and 25, this little horn makes war against the saints, speaks pompous words against God, intends to change times and law, and persecutes the saints for a "time and times and half a time" (literally three and a half years, but using the day-for-a-year principle of *Numbers 14:34* and *Ezekiel 4:6*, 1,260 years).

Evidence of this persecution can be seen through the centuries, as hundreds and thousands of people in Europe lost their lives through the inquisitions of the Roman Catholic judicial system. They were tortured for confessions of being heretics and killed because they would not submit to the authority and doctrines of the Roman Catholic Church and the pope.

Though the inquisitions of that time were abolished, the Bible indicates religious persecutions from the "little horn" will come back and result in the death of many before the return of Christ. Daniel also saw the conclusion concerning the "little horn," that when Jesus Christ returns, "the court [judgment] shall be seated, and they shall take away his dominion, to consume and destroy it forever" (verse 26; ***Revelation 18:2***)."

[1]The Kingdom of God

"The vision of ***Daniel 7*** could not end with any greater news: "Then the kingdom and dominion, and the greatness of the kingdoms under the whole heaven, shall be given to the people, the saints of the Most High. His kingdom is an everlasting kingdom, and all dominions shall serve and obey Him" (verse 27).

This prophecy ends by revealing that Jesus will establish the Kingdom of God on earth and give it to the saints of the Most High."

In the end we win. Become one of the saints by giving your life to Christ and entering the Kingdom of God.

[1]https://lifehopeandtruth.com/prophecy/understanding-the-book-of-daniel/daniel-7/. Author, Jim Haeffele. Retrieved from online source September 12, 2019.

CHAPTER FIVE
New Testament Dreams of the Lord

The Preservation of Jesus

After reading the dreams God communicated to his people in the New Testament, one thing is clear, the Dream of the Lord was very instrumental around Jesus and His birth. One of the first things we see in this saga is the preservation of the integrity of Mary, the mother of Jesus by a dream given to her future husband, Joseph. The dream is prophetic about the Messiah she carries, Jesus (*Matthew 1:18-23*).

In Ancient Israel, it was almost unheard of for a woman to bear children out of wedlock. It was most always a cause for stoning, ridicule and persecution by the religious of the day. Sometimes when God chooses us for an assignment, it can be very difficult socially, emotionally and otherwise, but God rewards our obedience to His call.

Mary was highly favored for this cause. She graciously

received, embraced and rejoiced after receiving the message brought by the angel, Gabriel (*Luke 1:26-28*). The message to her was that she was going to bear a Son by holy means. But for the times socially, she would be an outcast. However, God had a plan and needed to speak to her intended husband. In ancient Israel, the engagement almost literally meant an actual covenant of marriage.

Matthew 1:19-20

Then Joseph her husband, being a just man, and not willing to make her a public example, was minded to put her away privily.

But while he thought on these things, behold, the angel of the Lord appeared unto him in a dream, saying, Joseph, thou son of David, fear not to take unto thee Mary thy wife: for that which is conceived in her is of the Holy Ghost.

God needed Joseph to know His plan for Mary and the Baby she was carrying. He wanted him to know the truth so he would not abort his destiny or cause societal harm to Mary. So God gave him a dream that provided all the answers to his questions and beckoned him to finalize his marriage plans to her.

After Jesus was born, in alignment with the words of the Prophet Isaiah, the Baby and His mother were found in a manger because there was no room for them at the inn. This historical event was not hidden from mankind. The Bible declares there were men of wisdom who were aware of the Savior's birth through the stars in the heaven.

Matthew 2:1-2

[1]When Jesus was born in the village of Bethlehem in Judea, Herod was king. During this time some wise men from the east came to Jerusalem

[2]and said, "Where is the child born to be king of the Jews? We saw his star in the east and have come to worship him."

Herod secretly called the wise men and wanted to know when the sign of the Savior's birth first appeared in the sky. He wanted them to go to Bethlehem where he would have been born according to prophecy and find Him. The king pretended to want to go and worship Him too. When the wise men left the king, as they traveled, the star continued ahead of them and eventually lead to the place where the new born Savior could be found. There they worshipped and gave Him gifts.

Matthew 2:12

And being warned of God in a dream that they should not return to Herod, they departed into their own country another way.

Not only was Herod an evil king, but he was a lying one as well. Unbeknownst to the wise men, he really wanted to locate the new born king so He could be murdered.

The Dream of the Lord continues to prevail in the life of the baby Jesus. The wise men did not return to King Herod as he had desired, but were instructed to go home and not tell King Herod anything about the birth of Jesus.

Matthew 2:13-14

[13] When they had gone, an angel of the Lord appeared to Joseph in a dream. "Get up," he said, "take the child and his mother and escape to Egypt. Stay there until I tell you, for Herod is going to search for the child to kill him."

[14] So he got up, took the child and his mother during the night and left for Egypt, where he stayed until the death of Herod. And so was fulfilled what the Lord had said through the prophet: "Out of Egypt I called my son."

A dream from God can warn you of present danger and keep you safe. Even though the wise men did not return to him, King Herod knew Jesus had been born and wanted to kill Him. The warning Joseph received from this dream intervenes to protect the Savior yet again and fulfills ancient prophecy.

Matthew 2:19-21

[19] But when Herod was dead, behold, an angel of the Lord appeareth in a dream to Joseph in Egypt,

[20] Saying, Arise, and take the young child and his mother, and go into the land of Israel: for they are dead which sought the young child's life.

[21] And he arose, and took the young child and his mother, and came into the land of Israel.

Again, the Dream of the Lord comes to protect the baby Jesus and His parents. They were instructed to go Egypt temporarily to escape King Herod's deadly murder rampage of the infants in Israel. Now God informs Joseph of the king's death, which facilitates the environment of safety he needs to bring his family back to Israel. Yes, Joseph would have eventually learned of the king's death at some point, but it seems it was God's will he know as soon as possible.

These Dreams of the Lord combined are sent to protect the Savior and make way for His upbringing, ministry to the people and eventually death on the Cross.

The Dream of the Lord Reveals Innocence

The Chief priests and elders of the day had met to finish their plans to crucify Jesus. Then He was bound and delivered over to Pontius Pilate, the Roman governor, for further prosecution. They were unusually hardened against Him as is the case when satan is at work.

The Jewish leaders had made a political charge against Jesus claiming He criminally committed an act of treason against Caesar by claiming He was the King of the Jews. Their overall plan was to put Jesus to death according to the laws of Rome and free themselves of any guilt or condemnation knowing Jesus was innocent of this charge.

Jesus comes before Pontius Pilate after King Herod passes the buck of condemnation to him, because Herod could not bear to condemn Jesus himself. Pilate finds no evidence of treason in Jesus and appeals to the crowd and the powers that be for His release. He fervently asks them to release Jesus instead of Barabbas, a prisoner accused of murder. It was a Jewish custom to release a prisoner each year at Passover in these times, but the crowd chooses the murderer Barabbas instead.

Of all the rulers that administrated His crucifixion, Pilate was the one who seemed to experience true compassion for Jesus. In spite of the demonic pressure he was under, he desperately wanted to find a way to free Jesus from this most painful circumstance. Wrestling with the spirits of guilt and remorse, God sends confirmation of Pilate's gut feelings in a dream to his wife.

Matthew 27:19
When he was set down on the judgment seat, his wife sent unto him, saying, Have thou nothing to do with that just man: for I have suffered many things this day in a dream because of him.

Pilate was like some of us, our allegiance to Christ at some point causes us to risk our reputation, position, power and self-interest. He could not cope with the pressure. Unable to persuade the demonically oppressed crowd to plead for Jesus, he took water and washed his hands. Through this action he declared his own innocence as he condemned the sinless Son of God. The Dream of the Lord sears Pilate's conscience and yet affirms Jesus' innocence.

CHAPTER SIX
The Dream of the Lord Brings Prosperity

Isaiah 48:17
Thus says the Lord, your Redeemer, the Holy One of Israel: I am the Lord your God, Who teaches you to profit, Who leads you in the way that you should go.

There are times when the Lord will visit us with visions of prosperity and show us His pleasure with our prosperity. My father was most unfortunate to have been injured at his job in a Detroit factory. He lost the use of one of his hands. The accident was not his fault, but the fault of the controls on the machine he was working. He sued his employer in order to recover damages for his pain and suffering. The resulting litigation continued on for several years, almost a decade.

My mother reports one night before she and my father were to settle the case for their pain and suffering from the accident, she had a dream. She said Jesus visited her and smiled at her and then walked away. It was not long after she and my father received a very, very large check.

My mother was able to build her dream home and enjoy some of the finer things she had always wanted.

I believe the Lord loves all of His children and at times, can hardly wait to bestow His blessings upon them. It is at this point He decides to visit us in our dreams of the night and hint of the impending blessing to come.

There are other times when He wants to give His children very definite instructions about what to do and where to go in order to acquire wealth. All the gold and silver is His and cattle on a thousand hills the Bible says. He knows exactly where it can be found and delights to show us the way to it.

One such occasion came about when Jacob wanted to leave the service of Laban, his father-in-law. He had served him for fourteen years just to be able to marry his daughter Rachel. He loved her the minute he saw her at her father Laban's house. It was love at first sight.

After Jacob was able to marry Rachel, she bore Joseph, their son. Sometime after, Jacob wanted to leave the house of Laban and establish his own home for his family. Laban was very crafty and had cheated Jacob out of his earnings at least ten times over the years. After Jacob expressed his desire to leave, Jacob told Laban what he wanted for repayment.

Jacob was very specific because he knew the heart of Laban. He knew Laban would try and cheat him once again. He told him that he did not want anything from him, except to continue to care for the herds. Jacob made Laban an offer he could not refuse. He told Laban he would only take the cattle, sheep and goats that were speckled, spotted or brown. Afterwards Laban had his son's remove all of the herds that genetically matched Jacob's description. He felt assured Jacob had no chance of reproducing after this kind with no males or females with these characteristics for mating.

Laban knew and acknowledged his prosperity was due to the anointed hands and wisdom of his nephew Jacob. Jacob knew Laban would be reluctant to let him go peaceably and with the proper wages owed to him. But God revealed to Jacob in a dream what he should do to cause his herds to conceive the very thing he gave up. His herds were going to conceive and be speckled, spotted and ring-streaked offspring!

God instructed Jacob to peel the wood from poplar tree branches, revealing the white beneath. He also led Jacob to place the branches in the watering troughs, for the herds would mate after they drank. The result is all Jacob's herds reproduced spotted, speckled and ring-streaked, supernaturally, without natural DNA!

Genesis 30:39
The flocks bred and conceived in sight of the rods and brought forth lambs and kids streaked, speckled, and spotted.

Therefore Jacob outwitted Laban and created an abundance of herds he got to keep as his own. The God of Abraham, Isaac and Jacob had supernaturally provided for Jacob and his family. To further explain his unbelievable success to his wives, Jacob gave them an explanation about the dream he had (*Genesis 31:10-12*). The Bible declares in *Psalms 35:27* God takes pleasure in the prosperity of His servants. As it was with Jacob, so God will cause it to be with us.

A Personal Prosperity Dream of the Lord

I had a dream almost fourteen years ago. In the dream my father had died (which had already happened in 1981), followed by my mother. After this I was shown a book of blank checks with a Christmas logo on the front of them. This book of checks was drawn of my mother's checking account. It was the same account she had before her death.

The dream was so real I thought the Lord was telling me my mother was about to die. The blank checks made no sense to me whatsoever and I assumed it represented some kind of inheritance. When I saw the death of my mother was not yet forthcoming, I stored that dream in the back of my mind. As I have stated earlier in this book, you will never forget the dream of the Lord.

My mother did not pass away until September of 2014. My parents died almost 33 years apart. My mother became very ill and it became necessary that I take care of her.

Because of my obligation to her, I had become unemployed and without any means of support. When her death was indeed imminent, I began to ponder the meaning of the dream that had come to me so many years before. It was clear God was speaking to me about something financial.

Everyone knows checks are related to money, but blank checks were different, at least to me. I believe the one thing God knew about me is I would continue to investigate the symbolic meaning of those blank checks. Also I was not forgetting in the dream regarding those blank checks, a symbol indicating the Christmas season. I came to eventually understand blank checks are not money, but they represent a demand for money.

Finally, in the Christmas season of 2016, I believe this dream came true. I found out by accident my parents had stock in the local utility company. Both of my parents had now passed on. The electric company had a stock account in my parents' names for over forty years. We made a demand for payment of those stocks and had a wonderfully blessed holiday.

This money was needed at a very crucial time in my life. I kept wondering what was so important God would show me those checks almost fifteen years before I ever needed what they symbolized. The time this occurred was a season of financial testing and I believe the Holy Spirit wanted me to know I had been provided for. The Dream of the Lord was announcing prosperity!

The Dream of the Lord is a rare occurrence. I do believe as we are headed towards the return of our Lord, Jesus Christ, these dreams will increase, especially about our finances. I believe God will begin to glorify Himself through such dreams as He takes pleasure in our prosperity.

CHAPTER SEVEN
Introduction to Dreams and Visions

Genesis 15:1

After these things the word of the LORD came unto Abram in a vision, saying, Fear not, Abram: I am thy shield, and thy exceeding great reward.

Up to this point in his life, Abram had given much to others, not for price or reward and he was obedient to the Lord his God.

In the above scripture, it is assumed Abram, who would become Abraham, is awake, which occurs during a vision. This is the first recorded vision in the Bible. God visits him through this means of communication and assures him of His blessing and favor.

Scientists can't explain why we dream or have visions. They simply do not have an explanation for why some are prophetic or even reveal current circumstances. However, dreams and visions are designed so we hear directly from God Himself. This is why they can't scientifically explain this phenomenon.

Dreams and visions are supernatural events. They are poured out upon everyone, God's servants and their children, and their children's children and the wicked alike. Got a problem with a child or a family member? Ask God to give them a dream. Nothing can touch the soul like His visitation.

The Difference Between Dreams, Visions and Trances

Dreams

Dreams occur from the subliminal state during the REM sleep cycle. REM sleep is known as "rapid eye movement" sleep. It is one of the five stages of sleep humans experience at night and it is the stage of sleep in which people dream. The results of REM sleep are random, rapid movements of the eyes and even a paralysis of the muscles. Outside of the Holy Spirit resting upon you, this is the most predominant factor for receiving dreams.

There are other natural factors that can cause dreams, but a dream from the Lord Himself can only be caused by the Holy Spirit. No matter if you have sleep problems or not, when the Holy Spirit visits you, you will have a dream from the Lord.

Dreams and trances both occur in the area of the sleep world. At this point, you are motionless. Your eyes can be either open or closed. During dreams, the subliminal mind undergoes a sequence of sensations. Images or thoughts pass through the sleeping person's brain and manifest a dream.

Visions

Numbers 24:16:

the message of one who hears the words of God, who has knowledge from the Most High, who sees a vision from the Almighty, who bows down with eyes wide open:

During a vision, the receiver is awake. It works through a mental function, but it is of God; the person sees an image with brain waves and not the physical eye.

Trances

A trance is a stunned or dazed condition of mental abstraction. It resembles sleep, but the person is receiving information or having a supernatural experience.

Acts 11:4-5

⁴But Peter began, and expounded the matter unto them in order, saying,

⁵I was in the city of Joppa praying: and in a trance I saw a vision, a certain vessel descending, as it were a great sheet let down from heaven by four corners; and it came even unto me:

Possibly to be alone, the Apostle Peter was praying on the rooftop of Simon, the tanner's house, in the city of Joppa. Peter becomes hungry, falls into a trance, but he does not lose control of his senses. In this luminous state God shows Peter a sheet full of creepy animals.

Then there was a voice Peter heard that said "arise, kill and eat." This command was a complete opposite to the ceremonial demand to the Jews not to eat any creepy thing found in the Book of Leviticus. God was giving Peter a new directive for the newly formed Church.

The outcome of this trance represented God's direct authorization to break down the barriers between the Jews and the Gentiles. He accomplished this by placing one of the leaders of the early Church in a trance to translate His desire. God began this initiative through addressing food they both ate.

My own trance experience is a rather a disturbing one. However, it was still a trance. One night I was asleep or at least I thought I was. I felt my covers slowly withdraw from me. I knew it was happening, but I had no power to stop it. I was paralyzed.

I soon felt a pair of hands wrap themselves around my neck and squeeze. Then I, within the trance, wrapped my hands around a neck and squeezed, but I added "in the Name of Jesus!" Those hands quickly let go of my neck and vanished. I felt them no more!

This was a trance where I felt awake and asleep at the same time. Immediately after, I remember the sensation of coming out of a dream and yet it was totally different from the dream state. Anytime you encounter the spiritual world, you will me encompassed in a trance.

I was angry and I got up and told the devil to never enter

my bedroom again! I plead the Blood of Jesus and went back to sleep.

God is still communicating our future, warnings, revelations and instructions through dreams, visions and trances. These are still standard modes of God's messaging today.

CHAPTER EIGHT
False and Demonic Dreams

Jeremiah 23:32
Behold, I am against them that prophesy false dreams, saith the LORD, and do tell them, and cause my people to err by their lies, and by their lightness; yet I sent them not, nor commanded them: therefore they shall not profit this people at all, saith the LORD.

This scripture contains almost the entirety of the purpose of a false dream. The word *false* in this scripture is taken from the Hebrew word *sheqer,* pronounced *sheh'-ker* meaning an untruth; a sham; without a cause, deceitful, lying, false or vain. Here God is talking about the prophets who tell false dreams to the people, to deceive them and always to control them.

The Bible says the devil is the father of lies. He can send dreams to us as we sleep as well. This should not be the norm, but rather abnormal. Anyone who is suffering dreams from the demonic or false soulish realm is being attacked by the devil and should be ministered to.

66

A false or demonic dream can be defined by the following:

1. Contradiction to the Bible

Galatians 1:8
But though we, or an angel from heaven, preach any other gospel unto you than that which we have preached unto you, let him be accursed.

Valid dreams and visions should not violate that which can be already confirmed in the Bible (for instance, you are already married and have a dream you had an affair and married your neighbor (which would be adultery). For some people, this type of dream would be inspiration to commit adultery, but God would not inspire this.

I believe I have given you Word-based wisdom for identifying the Dream of the Lord. However, satan's greatest weapon is deception and he will try to deceive us in the last days. He knows his time is short. Please understand he will try to seduce you as an angel of light. Consider the following scriptures:

2 Corinthians 11:13-14
[13]For such men are false apostles [spurious, counterfeits], deceitful workmen, masquerading as apostles (special messengers) of Christ (the Messiah).
[14]And it is no wonder, for Satan himself masquerades as an angel of light;

2. Come as nightmares or dreams that terrorize you or cause fear

2Timothy 1:7
For God hath not given us the spirit of fear; but of power, and of love, and of a sound mind.

Nightmares are defined by Webster's dictionary as:

1. *An evil spirit formerly thought to oppress people during sleep*

2. *A frightening dream that usually awakens the sleeper*

3. *Something (such as an experience, situation, or object) having the monstrous character of a nightmare or producing a feeling of anxiety or terror*

Clearly, we see by Webster's definition something other than the Lord is causing nightmares and dreams of terror to occur in our sleep.

The Dream of the Lord is all about God's thoughts regarding a particular person, place or thing communicated through a dream. I used tell listeners on my recent radio broadcast, The Dream Interpreter, "Not every dream is from the Lord." People often tell me their dreams and sometimes immediately I know their dream is not of God.

There are dreams that result from other sources as well. Solomon, who was known for his wisdom, said the following regarding dreams:

Ecclesiastes 5:3
For a dream comes with much business and painful effort, and a fool's voice with many words.

Solomon is perhaps saying if you think about something long enough, you may dream about it at night. These are empty dreams that are useless and do not benefit the dreamer in any way. The result is a dream that is confusing and incoherent.

Ecclesiastes 5:7

For in a multitude of dreams there is futility and worthlessness, and ruin in a flood of words. But [reverently] fear God [revere and worship Him, knowing that He is].

Solomon is talking about those crazy dreams. These are those dreams you have when you have eaten too much pizza. There will be many times you will have a dream that makes no sense whatsoever. Scientists have declared that some of these night visions occur as a result of just plain old brain activity or daydreaming.

Your dreams can also be a result of soulish activity. The soul as defined in the Bible is composed of the mind, will and the emotions.

I Thessalonians 5:23

Now may the God of peace Himself sanctify you entirely; and may your spirit and soul and body be preserved complete, without blame at the coming of our Lord Jesus Christ.

God desires your soul to be whole. But sometimes wounds, bruises, even images you have seen can have an effect on your soul can cause nightmares and other dreams.

Sometimes if God is trying to warn you, the Dream of the Lord may feel like a nightmare or have the emotions of a nightmare. There may be that same intensity or urgency as you would experience in a nightmare, but it is not. The Dream of the Lord is different in that you will not be fearful or terrified, but perhaps you will be notified.

So if your dream has made you fearful or timid, then it is not the Dream of the Lord. In times past, I have been very upset about situations and sure enough, those same situations have shown up in my dreams.

3.   Dreams containing sexual content, inspiration or where you are molested

Galatians 5:19
Now the works of the flesh are manifest, which are these; Adultery, fornication, uncleanness, lasciviousness,

A young lady once asked me about a dream she had. She said the dream had nudity and sexual activity. I knew this was not the Dream of the Lord. God will not take the time to communicate with you about sexual activity, especially with someone you are not in covenant. He would not defile you with sin in any form, not ever, and certainly not in a dream.

However, He would communicate with you about the sin, but the Holy Spirit does not need to visually show you more sin in order to convict you so you can repent of sin.

He is a holy God and even His dream language is holy. I have heard of many a dream where a person was naked, such as Adam and Eve were in the Garden of Eden. But the Holy Spirit can and will show you your nakedness so you get the point. Your enemy, the devil, however, wants to defile you and suggest things that would come against your redeemed imagination and conscience.

I Peter 1:14-16 (AMP)
14[Live] as children of obedience [to God]; do not conform yourselves to the evil desires [that governed you] in your former ignorance [when you did not know the requirements of the Gospel].
15But as the One Who called you is holy, you yourselves also be holy in all your conduct and manner of living.
16For it is written, You shall be holy, for I am holy.

So you see, God will not send you a communication through a dream that would tempt you to disobey Him or stain your imagination.

4. Deny Jesus is Lord and the Gospel

John 14:6
Jesus saith unto him, I am the way, the truth, and the life: no man cometh unto the Father, but by me.

Any dream that denies Jesus is the Savior is a lie of the devil. These dreams are meant to confer doubt, especially to new believers and those who are not firm in their salvation. This is somewhat related to contradicting the Bible, but can be a little more deceptive as the devil wants to point you away from the true Savior.

Most non-Christian religions are often based upon fantasies of hallucinations and trances. Most cults and false religions are built on this kind of private revelation. The Word of God tells us to test the spirit of the revelation to see who the source is.

I John 4:1
Beloved, do not believe every spirit, but test the spirits to see whether they are from God, because many false prophets have gone out into the world.

The word *test* in the above scripture is from the Greek word *dokimazo*, pronounced *dok-im-ad'-zo*. Its meaning includes examining, discerning and proving something. In these last days we will need to do this with all revelation that seems a little off or unusual.

5. Bring Torment

Isaiah 29:7-8 (CEV)
[7]Every brutal nation that attacks Jerusalem and makes it suffer will disappear like a dream when night is over.
[8]Those nations that attack Mount Zion will suffer from hunger and thirst. They will dream of food and drink but wake up weary and hungry and thirsty as ever.

It seems these kinds of dreams arise out of fleshly appetites and bring torment such like a famished person would dream of food and water.

In general, yes, there can be false dreams, but if you diligently follow and compare your dream with the criteria I have set forth in this book and the Bible, you can safely assume you have been visited with the Dream of the Lord!

CHAPTER NINE
Biblical Dream Interpretation 101

Genesis 41:15
The king said to him, "I had a dream, yet no one can explain what it means. I am told that you can interpret dreams."

Every week on my radio broadcast, I would tell people: "God meant for all of us to interpret His dreams. The Bible declares in *2 Corinthians 5:10* we must all appear before the judgment seat of Christ. If we must all appear before Him, why would He hide from us the things He wants us to do? That is totally unreasonable from an all knowing, all powerful and merciful God.

The interpretation of the dream is intended solely for the dreamer. However, the dreamer may need help discovering the dream's meaning such as the case of Nebuchadnezzar, Pharaoh, the butler and the baker.

When you receive a Dream of the Lord, what should you do? The following scripture tells us:

Habakkuk 2:2
And the LORD answered me, and said, Write the vision, and make it plain upon tables, that he may run that readeth it.

1. Write it down.

The Lord told Habakkuk to write the vision down. Remember, dreams and visions of the Lord are very clear and concise events. You may not yet understand the very meaning of it, but only by duplicating the dream or vision in writing will you fully capture, describe and inscribe it.

2. Make it plain for others who may need to read it. In other words, explain what you saw.

3. Identify the major symbols and numbers in your dream and research biblical references to them.

   (a) Search for your symbol in your Biblical concordance for its context and meaning.

4. Share your dream or vision with those you trust and those who are familiar with the dream language of God.

5. Note personal points of interest or any past experiences in the dream.

6. Ignore old wives' tales about dreams.

   Some people will tell you if you dream a woman, it's a man, and if you dream it's a man, it's a woman. If you dream it's a death, it will be a birth in the family, if you dream it's a birth, it will be a death. God says what He means and means what He says. He will not try to confuse you.

7. Look up dictionary descriptions about dream elements

Sometimes a dictionary can make plain the purpose or function of something you see in your dream. A word definition can bring clarity and revelation.

8. Your dream can be interpreted by you or another anointed person.

Daniel 5:12
Forasmuch as an excellent spirit, and knowledge, and understanding, interpreting of dreams, and shewing of hard sentences, and dissolving of doubts, were found in the same Daniel, whom the king named Belteshazzar: now let Daniel be called, and he will shew the interpretation.

Hopefully, you are in the midst of someone who can help you interpret your dream correctly. The wonderful thing about the internet is the advent of social media. There are many sites out there with Christians helping each other to understand the dreams that God gives them and God is faithful.

James 1:5
[5]*If any of you is deficient in wisdom, let him ask of the giving God [Who gives] to everyone liberally and ungrudgingly, without reproaching or faultfinding and it will be given him.*

Rest assured the Helper, the Holy Spirit, is there to help you. He will respond to your request for wisdom when you ask Him. This is why Jesus sent Him back to earth. He will give you understanding, primarily because your obedience depends upon it.

9. Explore the biblical meanings and associations of significant elements in your dream.

Write down any numbers, colors and symbols that may be prominent in your dream and explore them in the Bible. Also document anything you hear, anything that is said, people you know and your feelings within the dream.

I have included the following prayer for revelation. Before God blessed me with understanding for dreams and visions, this was one the prayers I prayed often:

Father, in the name of Jesus I ask you for the spirit of revelation and understanding to rest upon me. I ask that You open my spiritual eyes, so I can see and my spiritual ears so I can hear what thus saith the Lord. I ask for understanding of all dreams and visions along with their interpretation. I thank you for this new anointing upon my life. Amen.

Pray this prayer regularly and I believe with you the spirit of revelation will come upon you for God-glorifying and accurate dream interpretation.

CHAPTER TEN
Biblical Meaning of Numbers in your Dream

Matthew 10:30

But the very hairs of your head are all numbered.

God uses something as insignificant as the number of hairs on our head to show He is even in control of even the smallest things. Numbers are important to us. They are everywhere. They represent our rank, our accounts, our turn, our money, our cars and even our houses. It is very natural for us to look at a number and determine something.

I was sitting on my bed one morning and it occurred to me God only uses numbers when He is also trying to make a point. Other than this, God is a God of infinity. He told Abraham the number of Israel would be limitless!

Genesis 15:5

And he brought him forth abroad, and said, Look now toward heaven, and tell the stars, if thou be able to number them: and he said unto him, So shall thy seed be.

So now biblical numerology makes sense. When God shows us a number in our dreams, He is defining something. He is truly giving us a message. It is when we observe the same number, surrounded by the same circumstances over and over again in the Bible we can safely establish its meaning.

Take for instance the number 7. The following scriptures bursting with its meaning:

Genesis 2:2
And on the seventh day God ended his work which he had made; and he rested on the seventh day from all his work which he had made.

Genesis 29:20
And Jacob served seven years for Rachel; and they seemed unto him but a few days, for the love he had to her.

Genesis 41:27
And the seven thin and ill favoured kine that came up after them are seven years; and the seven empty ears blasted with the east wind shall be seven years of famine.

We are able to see things happen after seven days, years, things, etc. We can assume seven is a number God uses for completeness and fullness. The number seven is divine.

Even our adversary's name is associated with a number

we all recognize as 666. If you saw this number in a dream or anywhere else, most people would recognize its meaning. After all of this biblical researching, we can still ask God Himself what a number means.

My favorite number is "333." I would see it on my clock when I awoke in the middle of the night. This number would be attached to sale items in the store and sometimes it would be on a check or a receipt. All I know is when I see that number, something wonderful is going to happen. It has always been God talking to me and telling me everything was going to be okay.

One example: I was going through a rather financial wilderness in my life. At the time I did not have a lot of money which forced me to believe God for everything every moment and to walk by faith.

I had to go sixty miles to a very important meeting. I had enough gas to get there and just a few dollars at my disposal to get back. I drove there by faith thinking I would preserve my gas by driving conservatively. I believed and I went.

Just before I got to where I was going, I came upon a car in front of me that had "333" contained in the license plate number. I knew after this, whatever was going to take place, it would be a manifestation of God. That particular day, it did not seem God manifested in my meeting in any particular way, but I still had this other miracle I needed.

As it happened, after driving conservatively, I still needed gas and my few dollars would not have netted me enough. I began to look for any fallen change in my car which turned out to be mostly pennies and small change. When I looked in my glove compartment, hoping against hope, money was in there, a ten dollar bill popped out! It was enough to get home. God had shown up once again! The number "333" was my sign.

The number "10" itself is the number of testimony. One of the definitions of the word *testimony* is proof. This miracle was proof God rewards faith, He will always provide your every need. Abundant life means having what you need at the exact moment you need it!

Eventually God would reveal to me the meaning of "333." It symbolizes the death, burial and resurrection of Jesus Christ! This number remains my personal reminder of God's faithfulness and comfort when I need it.

If I see this number in a dream, I know what it means to me. This is the way God uses numbers in your dreams. It is the way He uses numbers everyone knows the meaning of to send a message in dreams. Numbers in a dream are a definite major part of its interpretation.

Biblically, the number "seven" is considered a number of completeness of perfection or the Holy Spirit's work. Pharaoh's dream told to Joseph was populated with many sevens, which indicated the perfect length of time in each season Pharaoh was shown in his dreams.

The number "eight" signifies resurrection, regeneration or a new beginning. The eighth day signifies a new and first thing. The Jews were commanded to circumcise the male newborns on the eight day.

Genesis 17:12
From now on, your family must circumcise every baby boy when he is eight days old. You must even circumcise any man or boy you have as a slave, both those born in your homes and those you buy from foreigners. This will be a sign that my promise to you will last forever.

The following numbers correspond to meanings found in the Bible:

[1]Numbers and Their Biblical Meaning

Number	Meaning
1	Unity; New beginnings
2	Union; Division; Witnessing
3	Divine Completeness and perfection
4	Creation; The world; Creative works
5	Grace; God's goodness, Pentateuch
6	Weakness of man; Manifestation of sin; Evils of Satan
7	Resurrection; Spiritual completeness; Father's perfection
8	New Birth; New beginnings
9	Fruit of the Spirit; Divine completeness

Numbers Continued

10	Testimony; Law and responsibility
11	Disorder and Judgment
12	Governmental perfection
13	Apostasy; depravity and rebellion
14	Deliverance; Salvation; Change of Season
15	Rest
16	Love
17	Victory
18	Bondage
19	Faith
20	Redemption
21	Exceeding sinfulness of sin
22	Light
23	Death
24	The Priesthood
25	Repentance; the forgiveness of sins
26	The Gospel of Christ
27	Preaching of the Gospel
28	Eternal life
29	Departure
30	Blood of Christ; Dedication
31	Offspring
32	Covenant
33	Promise
34	Naming of a son

Numbers Continued

35	Hope
36	Enemy
37	The Word of the Father
38	Slavery
39	Disease
40	Trials; Probation; Testings; Judgment
42	Israel's oppression; first advent
44	Judgment of the World
45	Preservation
50	Holy Spirit; Pentecost
60	Pride
66	Idol worship
70	Punishment and restoration of Israel; Universality
100	Election; Children of the promise
119	Spiritual perfection and victory **7*17=119**
120	Divine period of probation
144	The Spirit guided life
200	Insufficiency
333	Death, Burial and Resurrection of Jesus Christ
600	Warfare
666	Antichrist
777	Christ
1000	Divine completeness and the Father's glory
4000	Salvation of the world through the Blood of the Lamb (those who choose between Christ and the Antichrist

Numbers Continued

6000	Deception of the Antichrist; Second Antichrist
7000	Final Judgment
144,000	Those numbered with Israel from the twelve tribes

These numbers are familiar to all of us. Collectively, they convey a generalization of meaning we have come to understand universally.

[1]God Counts. Author and website address currently unavailable. PDF previously retrieved from the internet November 12, 2015.

CHAPTER ELEVEN
Biblical Meaning of Colors in your Dream

Most people report dreaming in color. How boring would a dream be if it were in black and white? It is my personal opinion, the Holy Spirit gives you a dream in black and white for effect. Dreaming in black and white is basic in its interpretation: lifeless, old, antique and whatever adjective you can conjure. Dreaming with colors can have specific meaning from the Holy Spirit too!

The first color mentioned in the Bible is the color green.

Genesis 1:30
And to every beast of the earth, and to every fowl of the air, and to everything that creepeth upon the earth, wherein there is life, I have given every green herb for meat: and it was so.

The dictionary defines green as:

1. colors grass-colored: of a color in the spectrum between yellow and blue, like the color of grass

2. *having edible green leaves: consisting of or containing green leaves of vegetables, or a green salad*

In today's society, *green* has become to define a means to make less harmful or more sensitive to the environment.

The wife of a well-known healing evangelist had a dream of revival. She dreamed the following:

"On April 5th, 2012, I had a dream the Lord gave me that was very real and incredibly vivid. I saw two mantles come together, one blue and one green, and make a perfect blend. The mantle became teal. My friend texted me today saying that he saw a similar vision, and it reminded me of my dream."

Here we see colors are a major part of her dream. The wife stated she believed the blue mantle was heavenly revelation and prophetic which we see in the spirit, dreams, and visions. The mantle the prophet wore in biblical days was blue. She said she believed the green mantle she saw in the dream represented new life, prosperity and healing. This teal mantle was a symbol of the prophetic and healing ministry that would manifest in the coming revival during these last days.

Her dream reveals one more clue to interpreting color manifested in a dream. The combination of colors may be indicative of at least two meanings from the colors combined. This investigation may lead to even further revelation of the dream meaning.

Our first encounter with vivid color in the Bible is conveyed in the story about Joseph and his coat of many colors.

Genesis 37:3
Now Israel loved Joseph more than all his children, because he was the son of his old age: and he made him a coat of many colors.

Jacob, the patriarch of the twelve tribes of Israel, was Joseph's father. He dressed Joseph in a ornate coat of many colors. This royal-like garment was also prophetic of his later place in Egyptian history, though Jacob did not know it.

The indication was this coat was a beautiful and intricately made garment that would have been desired by anyone. Joseph was wearing conclusive and undeniable proof Jacob loved him above all of his brothers. This gift from Jacob identified him as the chief heir above all of them!

The only other reference to this type of garment in the scriptures is the occasion King David gave a robe like this to his daughter, Tamar. This would have represented her royal status. But, for Joseph, the wearing of this garment could have been the straw that broke the camel's back for his envious brothers.

Genesis 37:4
And when his brethren saw that their father loved him more than all his brethren, they hated him, and could not

speak peaceably unto him.

In my own dream from the Lord, as I have previously discussed, I was dressed in a rainbow-colored dress and putting on rainbow-colored shoes. The rainbow is not the symbol of the Pride Movement. It is first God's symbol of covenant between He and man. It is also a symbol of God's glory. This meaning will never change or be abolished. God used the rainbow to seal His promise to Noah and mankind:

Genesis 9:11-12 (CEV)
[11]*I promise every living creature that the earth and those living on it will never again be destroyed by a flood.*
[12]*The rainbow that I have put in the sky will be my sign to you and to every living creature on earth. It will remind you that I will keep this promise forever.*

As we biblically define the colors in our dream, we will discover the meaning why God is using them. Compare the colors in your dream with those in the table, taken from the Word of God along with its scriptural meaning.

Biblical Colors Table

Color	Figurative Of:	Scripture
White	Glory and Majesty	Daniel 7:9
		Revelation 20:11
	Purity, Glory	Revelation 1:14
	Victory	Revelation 6:2
	Completion	John 4:35

Black	Sorrow, Calamity	Joel 2:6
	Hell	Jude 13
	Heavy rain	I Kings 18:45
	Famine	Revelation 6:5
Green	Spiritual privileges	Jeremiah 11:16
	Spiritual life	Psalms 52:8
		Psalms 92:12-15
	New life	Genesis 1:30
Red (Crimson)	God's wrath	Psalms 75:8
	Atonement	Isaiah 63:2
	Persecution	Revelation 12:3
	Drunkenness	Proverbs 23:29
	Sinfulness	Isaiah 1:18
Purple	Royalty	Judges 8:26
	Wealth	Luke 16:19
	Luxury	Revelation 17:4
Blue	Divine revelations	Exodus 24:10
	Heavenly character	Exodus 28:31
Gold	Saints refined	Job 23:10
	Headship	Daniel 2:32
	Redeemed	2 Timothy 2:20
	Faith purified	I Peter 1:7
	Christ's doctrine	Revelation 3:18

Not every color is mentioned here. This table contains biblical references for basic colors that can be used as a foundation for interpreting dream colors, and countless combinations, and their probable meanings.

CHAPTER TWELVE
Other Ways God Speaks

Dreams are the most common way God speaks to us. We would be surprised to discover there are various ways God, through the Holy Spirit is speaking to us every day, especially if you are looking to hear His voice.

Not only can we learn to hear God, but He says in His Word we are to inquire of Him. The Bible declares to us to get wisdom.

Proverbs 4:7
Wisdom is the principal thing; therefore get wisdom: and with all thy getting get understanding.

God will give us wisdom if we ask from a posture of faith, but how are we going to receive it? What form will it come? The Bible states from two or three witnesses every word is established. So if you are trusting God to show you an important answer to a decision, you should have confirmation. In this way, God establishes the way we should go. He delights in telling you. Afterwards, we can give right answers and make right decisions.

I am sure you will agree with me we are the least capable of making the best decision for our lives. Why, because our sight, knowledge and understanding is limited. I take comfort in relying on an all-wise, all-powerful, all-knowing God to tell me the right decision, except all those I must make by faith. There is a difference. It's okay to ask the Lord if you so should go to school. If He confirms this, then it would be doubt to ask the Lord if He will provide what you need to go to school.

When you ask God for an answer for a decision, He will give you an answer based on His knowledge. He knows the past, all things present and the future of every situation, every heart and every intent. Is this not reason enough to allow Him to tell you which way to go? It is then up to you to proceed by faith with what He has said. So inquiring of the Lord takes faith too.

Therefore for the Christian, it is important to know all the ways God will speak to us, so we can hear and obey Him. I can't and won't limit how God will speak to you. He can do whatever pleases and will use every means possible to inform you when you ask.

Ways God Spoke in Times Past

Even though God does not speak to us in the following ways anymore, it is still important to know how He did speak and under what circumstances. We can always learn about God through what He has historically done.

1. Fire

Exodus 3:2
And the angel of the LORD appeared unto him in a flame of fire out of the midst of a bush: and he looked, and, behold, the bush burned with fire, and the bush was not consumed.

I believe when most people think of God speaking through fire in past biblical times, they remember Moses and God's burning bush. God's fiery, burning bush got Moses' attention and the form He took to speak to Moses. This was God's calling card for Moses' call into the ministry of delivering the children of Israel from Egypt.

2. Whirlwind

Job 38:1
Then the LORD answered Job out of the whirlwind, and said,

God answers Job out of and through the sound of the mighty wind. He corrects him for some of the things He has said amiss about Him. God then corrects Job's faulty friends by confirming his righteousness.

3. Animals

Numbers 22:28
And the LORD opened the mouth of the ass, and she said unto Balaam, What have I done unto thee, that thou hast smitten me these three times?

Are you so stubborn God has to use the shock of an animal speaking to you to get you to repent? Well, He did when He became very angry with Balaam the prophet for agreeing to curse Israel for King Balak. Even with the nation's idolatrous ways, God says Israel is the "apple of His eye" and does appreciate what Balaam is attempting to be on his way to do.

Ignoring God's directions and oppositions, God allows a donkey to rebuke Balaam three times for beating her as he attempts to mount and ride her to meet Balak.

4. Voice from a Cloud

Matthew 17:5
While he yet spake, behold, a bright cloud overshadowed them: and behold a voice out of the cloud, which said, This is my beloved Son, in whom I am well pleased; hear ye him. Jesus took Peter, James and John with Him to a very high mountaintop. Just by looking at Jesus in His human form, one could not see His divine glory. These three were His chief disciples. On this particular day before His crucifixion, they were chosen to see His glory before they would witness His agony.

Jesus was transfigured before them in power and glory. In this glorious state Moses and Elijah appeared to talk to Him. They were on earth the predecessors of the Father's glory. Suddenly, the shadow of bright cloud passed over them from which the Heavenly Father spoke: "This is my Son, hear Him!

God, the Father, was putting an exclamation point on the ministry of Jesus, accentuating their faith in Him.

The Most Common Ways God Speaks Now

1. Still, small voice

1Kings 19:12
And after the earthquake a fire; but the LORD was not in the fire: and after the fire a still small voice.

In my opinion, this is the main way God speaks to His people in the new Dispensation of Grace. The voice of the Holy Spirit is not loud or boisterous. It is quiet, gentle and sometimes persistent, but not for long Your continued disobedience to His voice will not result in pushiness. The Lord will allow you to experience the consequences of your own way.

When I initially invited Christ into my heart, one of the first things I pondered was how I would hear Him. Through experience after experience and failure after failure, I learned which voice was His speaking to me. His voice proved faithful and was consistent with His Word and fruitfulness.

2. Urim and Thummin

Ezra 2:63 (AMP)
[Zerubbabel] the governor told them they should not eat of the most holy things [the priests' food] until there should be a priest with Urim and Thummin [who by consulting these articles in his breastplate could know God's will in the matter].

Once the Holy Spirit revealed to me the way the Urim and Thummim worked, it has become one of my favorite means of inquiring of the Lord. I take advantage of it every day. I have a notebook full of inquiries for the Lord constantly because there are decisions to be made every day.

The Bible defines the Urim and Thummim as a set of emblems that are placed on the breastplate of the priest, over his heart, who stands before the Lord. Urim is for light and the Thummim is, by implication, for darkness (or the absence of light) which makes the pair perfect. Both, when activated or not, give an answer to a question the priest would ask God. One is for "yes" and the other is for "no." Each would light up as a response. Together they represent truth.

By faith, I appointed and anointed my phone as my Urim and Thummin. Ringing in response to a question at a specific time would indicate a "yes" answer. If I received no ringing at that same time, it would indicate a "no." I know it sounds a little far-fetched, but this is in accordance with how the priest did it in Ancient Israel. It is still God doing the activation! It works! As you begin to trust the Holy Spirit's responses, you will see He still reveals His will through this practice.

3. Audible Voice

Act 9:4
And he fell to the earth, and heard a voice saying unto him, Saul, Saul, why persecutest thou me?

I believe I have heard the audible voice of God only once my life. In fact, I was still an unbeliever. I was a full-fledged sinner. I had come home from a party. I was getting dressed for bed and I heard a voice that said "Come into My Kingdom." It was not loud or scary, but soft and affirmative and somehow I knew it was the Lord.

I was so foolish, I told the Lord "no." I had been out of my parents' house for approximately two years. They made my sister and I attend the local Methodist church since we were twelve. I hated it so much, I pretended to be sick so I would not have to go. In my opinion, most of the Christians there were no different than anyone else outside the church.

The head deacon was the local nightclub owner. When there was a funeral, wailing family members would try to climb in the casket with their loved ones. This is how I learned to perceive an almighty God. Nothing matched the Bible I occasionally read. I wanted no part of church.

They were doing what they thought was best for us as good parents. However, I had said I was never going back to church once I left home. Looking backing it was pure folly and religion, I hated it. However, God had other ideas and spoke to me that night. He is so very patient. Three years later I was begging God to come into His kingdom!

4. Songs

Job 35:10
But none saith, Where is God my maker, who giveth
songs in the night;

I have had a lot of experiences in my thirty-five years of salvation in which God spoke to me through a song. However, there is one time I will not forget. I was going through a hard financial time. I was teaching Microsoft computer classes at a local school district. I was not making much money, but continuing to go forward and trust God. I tell a story in another book I have written how God engineered my application for a job I absolutely had no experience. It paid much, much better and was closer to my house.

On the way to my computer job one morning I turned on the radio. It was tuned to a secular station. The next song to play was Phyllis Hyman's "You Know How to Love Me." It was as if the Holy Spirit hit me like a ton of bricks. I began to weep and rejoice exceedingly. I could not believe the Lord was moving to this secular song! I wept and rejoiced until the song went off and I arrived in my job's parking area. I was stunned!

When I got inside, a co-worker handed me $300.00 and told me God told her to bless me. I also got a phone call from the employer offering me the job for which I had no experience! God knew how to love me and was letting me know it through this song!

5. Rhema

Hebrews 4:12 (CEV)

What God has said isn't only alive and active! It is sharper than any double-edged sword. His word can cut through our spirits and souls and through our joints and marrow, until it discovers the desires and thoughts of our hearts

God's Word is living and active. This means it can speak to us every day for every situation at any time. Not only for just casual browsing or learning, but we can ask God for a rhema, a "right-now" word and He will bless us with a word for our present situation.

A rhema word comes forth, it comes alive to you, and it stands out when you are reading the Word of God. Also, you can ask the Lord by faith for a rhema regarding a situation and receive it randomly from the Word. God will be faithful to give you what you need for that moment.

6. Prophetic Ministry

1Corinthians 14:3

But he that prophesieth speaketh unto men to edification, and exhortation, and comfort.

Prophetic ministry is supernatural through the Holy Spirit. When God speaks through someone, who does not know you, and he or she tells you about something for your future, something about your past or current situation, it is powerful.

This event should comfort, inspire and confirm things for you. As God's people we should have this ministry on a regular basis. God is still sending his prophets to hear His voice and communicate to you what He is saying today. We are to judge prophesy to confirm it is the Spirit of God. We should listen, examine with a pure heart and then submit it to God. A person ministering from the wrong spirit can cause us to err as well. However, a true word from God will come to pass.

7. Repetition

2 Corinthians 13:1
This is the third time I am coming to you. In the mouth of two or three witnesses shall every word be established.

Witness after witness can be God confirming a certain action, decision or fact you. I was restless and perhaps a little bored one evening. It was one of those nights where nothing of interest to me was on television.

That night I turned to a Christian station I usually do not watch, as I have other channels which are my favorites. The programming featured a doctor giving a testimony about how God naturally healed his mother of cancer.

My thought at that moment was "I have to look him up on the internet to see what other medical advice he may have." I did just that, but what I saw did not seem to address questions I had about another medical issue.

Within the same week on a Friday night, I briefly browsed the programming on my television for that night. I was looking to record anything interesting because I was going to be in a prayer service that same evening.

The same doctor, who I had never seen on television, was featured on a program on my local public station. From all the events regarding him I experienced that same week, I knew God wanted me to watch his program. He was going to say something I needed to hear!

8. The Answer "No"

Romans 8:28
And we know that all things work together for good to them that love God, to them who are the called according to his purpose.

Truly I have learned to appreciate God saying "no" in response to a question I have asked Him. It can be very disappointing to us when He says no, but very revealing. Just by giving us this answer we can be assured He has our very best interest at heart. I have come to appreciate His "no's" just as much as I enjoy a "yes" from Him.

I recently inquired to God about joining myself with a particular ministry. The church was a little farther away from my home and it would require some sacrifice to attend there, but I was willing. It is an international ministry that holds revival meetings all over the world.

I visited the actual ministry over the summer and I had such a good, Holy ghost time! It felt good to be around the people of God. Everyone I encountered was wonderful.

I found God's answer of "no" to be a little puzzling and disappointing. I finally thought maybe it was too far away to faithfully participate in any of the activities there and let it go.

Lately, there has appeared information on the internet from major Church leaders warning about the conduct of this church's pastor, which was quite disturbing. When I attended this church, the pastor was not there and did not conduct any services. However, the atmosphere and the people that were there was still a blessing to me.

I love the spirit of this church, but now I can see why God told me "no." The disobedience of one man can't stop His glory, but I trust His wisdom about the matter.

APPENDIX ONE
Biblical Symbolism Index

A	Figurative Of:	Scripture
Adder	Wickedness of sinners	Psalm 58:3,4
Agitation	The wicked	Isaiah 57:20
Agony	Spiritual striving	Colossians 1:29
	Laborious prayer	Colossians 4:12
Agriculture	Gospel seed	Matthew 13:1-9
	God's workers	John 36:36-38
	God's Word	Isaiah 55:10,11
	Final harvest	Mark 4:28:29
Airplane	People of the Church	Ephesians 2:6
Almond	Old age	Ecclesiastes 12:5
Altar	Sacrifice	Genesis 8:20
Animals	Universal peace	Isaiah 11:6-9
	Man's inner nature	Jeremiah 13:23
	World empires	Daniel 7:2-8
	Satanic powers	Revelation 12:4, 9
	Christ's sacrifice	I Peter18-20
Ant	Industry	Proverbs 6:6-8
		Proverbs 30:24, 25
Apparel	Christ's blood	Isaiah 63:1-3
	Christ's righteousness	Zachariah 3:1-5

Linda Sharon Sanders

Apparel Continued

	The Church's purity	Psalm 45:13,14
Aprons	Miraculous healing	Acts 19:12
Archers	Invincibility	Genesis 49:23
	The Lord's discipline	Job 16:13
	Loss of glory	Isaiah 21:17
	Divine judgment	Jeremiah 50:29
Arise (stand up)	Regeneration	Luke 15:18,20
	Resurrection	Matthew 9:25
	A miracle	Luke 4:39
Arrows	God's judgments	Deuteronomy 32:23, 42
	Intense affliction	Job 6:4
	Wicked intentions	Psalm 11:2
	Bitter words	Psalms 64:3
	God's power	Psalms 76:3
	Daily hazards	Psalms 91:5
	Children	Psalms 127:4
	A false witness	Proverbs 25:18
Ashes	Frailty	Genesis 18:27
	Destruction	Ezekiel 28:18
	Victory	Malachi 4:3
	Worthlessness	Job 13:12
	Transformation	Isaiah 61:3

Ashes Continued

	Vanity	Isaiah 44:20
	Afflictions	Psalms 102:9
	Destruction	Jeremiah 6:26
Ass (donkey)	Wildness	Genesis 16:12
	Stubbornness	Hosea 8:9
	Promiscuity	Jeremiah 2:24
Assembly	Congregation	Exodus 12:6
	Church	Hebrews 12:23
	Gathering	Numbers 8:9
Automobile (Chariot)	Characteristic of one's life	2 Kings 13:14
Axe	Judgment	Matthew 3:10
	Wrath	Jeremiah 51:20-24
	God's authority	Isaiah 10:15

B

Baby	Unenlightened	Romans 2:20
	True believers	Matthew 11:25
	New Christians	I Peter 2:2
	Fleshly Christians	I Corinthians 3:1
Bag	True righteousness	Proverbs 16:11
	True riches	Luke 17:33
	Insecure riches	Haggai 1:6

Baker	Evil spirit	Hosea 7:4-7
Balances	God's justice	Job 31:6
	God's judgment	Daniel 5:27
	Man's tribulation	Revelation 6:5
Bankruptcy	Individual condition	Philippians 3:4-8
Banner	Jehovah's name	Exodus 17:15
	God's salvation	Psalms 20:5
	God's Protection	Song of Solomon 2:4
	God's Power	Song of Solomon 6;4
Baptism	Regeneration	John 3:3, 5,6
	Cleansing	Acts 22:16
		Titus 3:5
Bear	Fierce revenge	2 Samuel 17:8
	Wicked rulers	Proverbs 28:15
	World empire	Daniel 7:5
	Final antichrist	Revelation 13:2
	Messianic times	Isaiah 11:7
Bed	The grave	Job 17-13-16
	Divine support	Psalms 41:3
	World security	Isaiah 57:7
Bells	Consecration	Zechariah 14:20
Binding (Tying)	Fixed agreement	Numbers 30:2
	God's Word	Proverbs 3:3

Binding (Tying) Continued

	The afflicted	Isaiah 61:1
	Satan	Luke 13:16
	The wicked	Matthew 13:30
	Keys of the Kingdom	Matthew 16:19
	A determined plan	Acts 20:22
	Marriage	Romans 7:2
Birds	Escape from evil	Psalms 124:7
	A wanderer	Proverbs 27:8
	Snares of death	Ecclesiastes 9:12
	Cruel kings	Isaiah 46:11
	Hostile nations	Jeremiah 12:9
	Wicked rich	Jeremiah 17:11
	Kingdom of heaven	Matthew 13:32
Blood	Sin	Isaiah 59:2, 3
	Cruelty	Habakkuk 2:12
	Abominations	Isaiah 66:3
	Guilt	2 Samuel 1:16
	Vengeance	Ezekiel 35:6
	Retribution	Isaiah 49:25, 26
	Slaughter	Isaiah 34:6-8
	Judgment	Revelation 16:6
	Victory	Psalms 58:10

Boiling	Trouble	Job 30:27
Bottle	God's remembrance	Psalms 56:8
	God's judgment	Jeremiah 13:12-14
	Sorrow	Psalms 119:83
	Impatience	Job 32:19
Bow (used to shoot arrows)	Strength	Job 29:20
	The tongue	Psalms 11:2
	Defeat	Hosea 1:5
	Peace	Hosea 2:18-19
Bowing the knee	Prayer	I Kings 8:54
	Homage	2 Kings1:13
	Repentance	Ezra 9:5-6
	Worship	Psalms 95:6
	Submission	Ephesians 3:14
		Philippians 2:10
Bracelets	Worldliness	Isaiah 3:19
Branch (a limb)	Heathen king	Daniel 11:7
	Israel	Romans 11:16, 21
	The Messiah	Isaiah 11:1
	Christians	John 15:5,6
	Prosperity	Proverbs 11;28
	Adversity	Job 15:32

Brass	Obstinate sinners	Isaiah 48:4
	Endurance	Jeremiah 15:20
	God's decrees	Zechariah 6:1
	Christ's glory	Daniel 10:6
Breach (a break)	Broken promises	Numbers 13:34
	Broken relations	2 Samuel 6:8
	Sin	Isaiah 30:13
	Spiritual decay	Isaiah 30:26
Bread	Christ	John 6:33-35
	Christ's death	I Corinthians 11:23-28
	Communion w/Christ	Acts 2:46
		I Corinthians 10:17
	Extreme poverty	Psalms 37:25
	Affliction	Isaiah 30:20
	Wickedness	Proverbs 4:17
	Sloth	Proverbs 31:27
Breastplate	Health	Job 21:24
Bride	Israel	Ezekiel 16:8-14
	Church	Revelation 21:2, 9
Bridegroom	God	Ezekiel 16:8-14
	Christ	Revelation 21:2, 9
Bridle	God's control	Isaiah 30:28
	Self-control	James 1:26

Bridled Continued

	Imposed control	Psalms 32:9
Briars	Sinful nature	Michal 7:4
	Change of nature	Isaiah 55:13
	Rejection	Isaiah 5:6
Brooks (streams)	Wisdom	Proverbs 18:4
	Prosperity	Job 20:17
	Deception	Job 6:5
	Refreshment	Psalms 110:7
Brother	An ally	Amos 1:9
	A spiritual companion	1 Corinthians 1:1
Bruising	Evils	Isaiah 1:6
	Weaknesses	2 Kings 18:21
	The afflicted	Luke 4:18
	The Messiah's pains	Isaiah 53:5
	Satan's defeat	Romans 16:20
Buckler (shield)	The Lord	Psalms 18:2, 30
	God's truth	Psalms 91:4
	God's help	Proverbs 2:7
Bull	Evil men	Psalms 22:12
	Mighty men	Psalms 68:30
	Lord's sacrifice	Isaiah 34:6, 7
	Strength	Deuteronomy 33:17

Burden	Care	Psalms 55:22
	Prophet's message	Habakkuk 1:1
	Rules, Rites	Luke 11:46
	Sin	Psalms 38:4
	Responsibility	Galatians 2:2, 5
Butter	Smooth words	Psalms 55:21

C

Cake	Defeat	Judges 7:13
	Weak religion	Hosea 7:8
Caldron (a large kettle)	Safety	Ezekiel 11:3, 7, 11
Calf	Praise	Hosea 14:2
	Saints sanctified	Malachi 4:2
	Patience	Ezekiel 1:7
Camp	God's people	Revelation 20:9
Candle	Conscience	Proverbs 20:27
	Prosperity	Job 29:3
	Industry	Proverbs 31:18
	Death	Job 18:6
	God's justice	Zephaniah 1:12
Candlestick	Christ	Zachariah 4:2, 11
	The Church	Revelation 1:13, 20

Captive	Those under satan	2 Timothy 2:26
	Those under sin	2 Timothy 2:6
	Liberated by Christ	Luke 4:18
Carcass (a dead body)	Those in hell	Isaiah 66:24
	Idolatrous kings	Ezekiel 43:7, 9
	Attraction	Matthew 24:28
Cart	Sin	Isaiah 5:18
Castration	Absolute devotion	Matthew 19:12
Cedar (evergreen tree)	Israel's glory	Numbers 24:6
	Christ's glory	Ezekiel 17:22, 23
	Growth of saints	Psalms 92:12
	Mighty nations	Amos 2:9
	Arrogant rulers	Isaiah 2:13
Ceiling	Wealth	Jeremiah 22:14
Celibacy	Absolute devotion	Revelation 14:4
Chain	Oppression	Lamentations 3:7
	Sin's bondage	Psalms 68:6
	Punishment	2 Peter 2:4
	Satan's defeat	Revelation 20:1
Chamber,(Inner room)	Heavens	Psalms 104:3, 13
	Protection	Isaiah 26:20
	Evil practices	Ezekiel 8:12
	Lewdness	Romans 13:13

Chamber (Inner room) Continued

	Death	Proverbs 7:27
Chariot (Automobile)	Clouds	Psalms 104:3
	God's judgments	Isaiah 66:15
	Angels	2 Kings 6:16, 17
	One's Life	2 Kings 13:14
Cheekbone	Victory	Psalms 3:7
Cheese	Trials	Job 10:10
Childhood	Dependence	1 Thessalonians 2:7
	Immaturity	1 Corinthians 13:11
	Foolishness	Proverbs 22:15
	Unstableness	Ephesians 4:14
	Humility	Matthew 18:1-5
	Need for instruction	Proverbs 22:6
	Influence on adults	Isaiah 49:15
Children	Students of a teacher	Mark 10:24
	Christians	Ephesians 5:8
Circle	Used of the earth	Isaiah 40:22
Cistern (underground reservoir)	Wife	Proverbs 15:5
	Heart	Ecclesiastes 12:6
	False religion	Jeremiah 2:13

Clay	Man's weakness	Isaiah 64:8
	Unstable government	Daniel 2:33-35, 42
	Wealth	Habakkuk 2:6
	Trouble	Psalm 40:2
Cloak	Covering for sin	John 15:22
Clean	Repentance	Genesis 35:2
	Regeneration	Ezekiel 35:2
	Sanctification	Psalms 24:4
	Glorification	Revelation 19:8, 14
Closet	Place of prayer	Matthew 6:6
Cloud	God's Unsearchableness	Psalms 97:2
	Sins	Isaiah 44:22
	God's glory	I Kings 18:11
	Impending rain	I Kings 18:44
	Witnesses	Hebrews 12:1
	False teachers	2 Peter 2:17
	Baptism	1 Corinthians 10:1-2
Coal (Charcoal)	Lust	Proverbs 6:25, 28
	Purification	Isaiah 6:6
	Good deeds	Romans 12:10
	Posterity	2 Samuel 14:7

Coffin	Physical death	Genesis 50:26
Cold (absence of heat)	God's power	Psalms 147:17
	Laziness	Proverbs 20:4
	Good news	Proverbs 25:25
	Rejection of faith	Jeremiah 18:14
	Spiritual decay	Matthew 24:12
Congregation	A religious assembly	Acts 13:43
Corn	Blessings	Ezekiel 36:29
	Heavenly food	Psalms 78:24
	Christ	John 12:24
	Life's maturity	Job 5:26
Cross	Duty	Matthew 10:38
	Christ's sufferings	Ephesians 6:16
	The Christian faith	I Corinthians 1:18
	Reconciliation	Ephesians 2:16
Crown	A good wife	Proverbs 12:4
	Old age	Proverbs 16:31
	Children	Proverbs 17:6
	Honor	Proverbs 27:24
	Material blessings	Psalms 65:11
	Christ	Psalms 132:18
	Christ at His return	Revelation 19:12
	Christ glorified	Hebrews 2:7, 9

Crown Continued

	The Church	Isaiah 62:3
	The Christian's reward	2 Timothy 2:5
	Soul winners	1 Thessalonians 2:19
	The Christian's prize	I Corinthians 9:25
Crucifixion	Utter rejection	Hebrews 6:6
	Denial of faith	Revelation 11:8
	Union with Christ	Galatians 2:20
	Separation	Galatians 6:14
	Sanctification	Romans 6:6
	Dedication	1 Corinthians 2:2
Crumbs	Poverty	Luke 16:21
Crying	Remorse	Hebrews 12:17
	Pretense	Judges 14:15-18
	Sorrow	2 Samuel 18:33
	Other's sins	Psalms 119:136
	Pain	Hebrews 5:7
Crystal	Heaven	Revelation 4:6
Cup	One's portion	Psalms 11:6
	Blessings	Psalms 23:5
	God's wrath	Isaiah 51:17
	Suffering	Matthew 20:23
	Hypocrisy	Matthew 23:25-26
	New covenant	I Corinthians 10:16

Curtains	The heavens	Psalms 104:2
Cymbal	Pretense	I Corinthians 13:1
D		
Dance	Victory	I Samuel 6, 7
	Rejoicing in the Lord	2 Samuel 6:14-18
	Lust	Matthew 14:6
Darkness	God's unsearchableness	Psalms 97:2
	The way of sin	Ephesians 5:11
	Afflictions	Psalms 112:4
	Satan's dominion	Colossians 1:13
	Moral depravity	Romans 13:12
	Ignorance	1 John 2:8-11
	Death	Job 10:21-22
	Misery, Trouble	Job 37:19
	Uncertainty	1 Samuel 22:29
	Hell	Matthew 22:13
Daytime	Believers	1 Thessalonians 5:5, 8
	Christ's return	1 Thessalonians 5:2
	Prophetic period	Daniel 12:11
		Revelation 2:10
	Eternity	Daniel 7:9, 13
	Present age	Hebrews 1:2

Dead	Unbelievers	Ephesians 2:1
	Unreal faith	James 2:17, 19
	Decadent Church	Revelation 3:1
	Legal requirements	Hebrews 9:14
	Freedom from sin	Romans 6:2, 8, 11
	Freedom from religious law	Romans 7:4
Deaf	Patience	Psalms 38:13
Debt	Sins	Matthew 6:12
	Works	Romans 4:4
	Moral obligation	Romans 1:14
Deluge (the flood)	Power of God	Isaiah 59:19
	Baptism	1 Peter 3:20, 21
	Christ's coming	Matthew 24:36-39
	Destruction	Isaiah 28:2, 18
	The end	2 Peter 3:5-15
Dew	God's blessings	Genesis 27:28
	God's truth	Deuteronomy 32:2
	The Messiah	Isaiah 26:19
	Peace and harmony	Psalms 133:3
Diadem (crown)	Reward	Job 29:14
	For God's people	Isaiah 28:5

Diadem (Crown) Continued

	God's people	Isaiah 62:3
Dogs	Promiscuity	Deuteronomy 23:18
	Contempt	1 Samuel 17:43
	Worthlessness	2 Samuel 9:8
	Satan	Psalms 22:20
	Unbelievers	Matthew 7:6
	Gentiles	Matthew 15:26
	False teachers	2 Peter 2:22
	The lost	Revelation 22:15
Door	Christ	John 10:7, 9
	Christ's return	Matthew 24:33
	Day of salvation	Matthew 25:10
	Opportunity	2 Corinthians 2:12
Dove	Loveliness	Song of Solomon 2:14
	Desperate mourning	Isaiah 38:14
	Holy Spirit	Matthew 3:16
	Harmlessness	Matthew 10:16
Dragon	Satan	Revelation 12:9
	Antichrist	Revelation 12:3
Drink	Famine	2 Kings 18:27

Drink Continued

	Misery	Isaiah 51:22
	Married pleasure	Proverbs 5:15
	Unholy alliances	Jeremiah 2:18
	God's blessings	Zachariah 9:15-17
	Spiritual communion	John 6:53, 54
	Holy Spirit	John 7:37-39
Drought	Spiritual barrenness	Jeremiah 14:1-7
Drunkenness	Destruction	Isaiah 49:26
	Error	Isaiah 28:7
	Spiritual blindness	Isaiah 29:9-11
	International chaos	Jeremiah 25:15-29
	Persecution	Revelation 17:6
Dumb (speechless)	Calamity	Psalms 38:13
	God's judgments	Psalms 32:2-9
	Submissiveness	Isaiah 53:7
	Inefficient leaders	Isaiah 56:10
	Helplessness	I Corinthians 12:2
	Silence	Psalms 39:2
Dung (excrement)	Something worthless	2 Kings 9:37
	Ruin	Daniel 2:5
	Uncleanness	Malachi 2:3
	Man's righteousness	Philippians 3:8

Dunghills	Wretched condition	Psalms 113:7
Dust	Man's morality	Genesis 3:19
	Great multitude	Genesis 13:16
	Judgment	Deuteronomy 28:24
	Act of cursing	2 Samuel 16:13
	Dejection	Job 2:12
	Subjection	Isaiah 49:23
	The grave	Isaiah 26:19
	Rejection	Matthew 10:14
E		
Eagle	God's care	Exodus 19:4
	Swift armies	Jeremiah 4:13
	Spiritual renewal	Isaiah 40:31
	Flight of riches	Proverbs 23:5
	False security	Jeremiah 49:16
	Roman army	Matthew 24:15, 28
Earrings	Worldliness	Genesis 35:2-4
Earthquake	God's power	Hebrews 12:26
	God's presence	Psalms 68:7, 8
	God's Anger	Psalms 18:7
	God's judgments	Isaiah 24:18-21
Eyes of God	Omniscience	2 Chronicles 16:9
	Justice	Amos 9:8

Eyes of God Continued

	Holiness	Habakkuk 1:13
	Guidance	Psalms 32:8
	Protection	Psalms 33:18
Eyes of Man	Revealed knowledge	Numbers 24:3
	Lawlessness	Judges 17:6
	Jealousy	1 Samuel 18:9
	Understanding	Psalms 19:8
	Agreement	Isaiah 52:8
	Great sorrow	Jeremiah 9:1
	Retaliation	Matthew 5:38
	Spiritual inability	Matthew 13:15
	Spiritual dullness	Mark 8:17, 18
	Future glory	I Corinthians 2:9
	Illumination	Ephesians 1:18
	Unworthy service	Ephesians 6:6
	Worldliness	1 John 2:16
	Evil desires	2 Peter 2:14

F

Fan	God's judgments	Isaiah 30:24
	Nation's judgments	Jeremiah 51:2
	Christ's judgments	Matthew 3:12
Father	Source	Job 38:28

Father Continued

	Original inventor	Genesis 4:20
	Creator	James 1:17
	Spiritual likeness	John 8:44
	Counselor	Genesis 45:8
	Superior	2 Kings 2:12
Feed	Instruction and care	2 Samuel 5:2
	Spiritual provision	John 21;15-17
	Messiah	Ezekiel 34:23
	Good deeds	Matthew 25:37
	Supernatural supply	Revelation 12:6
	Elemental teaching	1 Corinthians 3:2
	Change of nature	Isaiah 11:7
	Corruption	Psalms 49:14
	Vanity	Hosea 12:1
	Eternal provision	Revelation 7:17
Feet	God's messengers	Roman 10:15
Fetters (shackles)	Trouble	Job 36:8
	Subjection	Psalms 149:8
Field	World	Matthew 13:38, 44
	Harvest	John 4:35
Finger	God's power	Exodus 8:19
	Inspiration	Exodus 31:18

Finger Continued

	Suggestiveness	Proverbs 6:13
	Lord's authority	Luke 11:20
Fire	God's protection	Zachariah 2:5
	God's vengeance	Hebrews 12:29
	God's word	Jeremiah 5:14
	Christ	Malachi 3:2
	Holy Spirit	Acts 2:3
	Angels	Hebrews 1:7
	Tongue	James 3:6
	Persecution	Luke 12:49-53
	Affliction	Isaiah 43:2
	Purification	Isaiah 6:5-7
	Love	Song of Solomon 8:6
	Lust	Proverbs 6:27, 28
Firebrand (torch)	Enemies	7:4
Fish	Men in the sea of life	Ezekiel 47:9, 10
	Ignorant men	Ecclesiastes 9:12
	Prison	Jonah 1:17
	Miraculous provision	Matthew 17:27
Flood	Ungodly men	2 Samuel 22:5
	Great trouble	Psalms 32:6
	An enemy	Isaiah 59:19

Flood Continued

	An invading army	Jeremiah 46:7, 8
	Great destruction	Daniel 9:26
	Testing	Matthew 7:25, 27
	Persecution	Revelation 12:15-16
Flowers	Christ's graces	Song of Solomon 5:13
	Shortness of life	Job 14:2
	Israel	Isaiah 28:1
	Man's glory	James 1:10-11
Foot	Obedience	Deuteronomy 33:3
	Instruction	Acts 22:3
	Teachable	Luke 10:39
Footstool	Earth	Matthew 5:35
	Ark	1 Chronicles 28:2
	Temple worship	Psalms 99:2
	Subjection	Acts 2:35
Forehead	Shamelessness	Revelation 17:5
	Stronger power	Ezekiel 3:8-9
	Devotion to God	Ezekiel 9:4
	Disrespectful	2 Chronicles 26:19
	Christ's true servants	Revelation 7:3
Forest	Army	Isaiah 10:18-19

Forest Continued

	Kingdom	Jeremiah 21:14
	Unfruitfulness	Jeremiah 26:18
		Hosea 2:12
Foundation	Christ	Isaiah 28:16
		Matthew 16:18
	Christian truth	Ephesians 2:20
	God decrees	2 Timothy 2:19
	Security of parents	1 Timothy 6:19
	The eternal city	Hebrews 11:10
Fowler (one who catches birds)	False prophets	Ezekiel 13:4
	Temptations	Psalms 91:3
		Psalms 124:7
Fox	False prophets	Ezekiel 13:4
	Enemies	Song of Solomon 2:15
	Deceivers	Luke 13:32
Frog	Unclean spirits	Revelation 16:13
Frost	God's creative ability	Job 38:29
Fruit	Repentance	Matthew 3:8
	Industry	Proverbs 31:16, 31
	Christian graces	Galatians 5:22-23
	Holy life	Proverbs 11:30

Fruit Continued

	Christian converts	John 4:36
	Christ	Psalms 132:11
	Sinful life	Matthew 7:16
	Reward of righteousness	Philippians 1:11
Furnace (hot fire)	Spiritual refinement	Psalms 12:6
	Lust	Hosea 7:4
	Hell	Matthew 13:42, 50
	Punishment	Ezekiel 22:18-22

G

Garden	Desolation	Amos 4:9
	Fruitfulness	Isaiah 51:3
	Prosperity	Isaiah 58:11
	Righteousness	Isaiah 61:11
Gate	Satanic power	Matthew 16:18
	Death	Isaiah 38:10
	Righteousness	Psalms 118:19-20
	Salvation	Matthew 7:13
	Heaven	Revelation 21:25
Ghost	Death	Genesis 35:29
		Mark 15:37
Girdle (belt)	Strength	Isaiah 22:21
	Gladness	Psalms 30:11

Girdle (Belt) Continued

	Truth	Ephesians 6:14
	Readiness	Luke 12:35
		I Peter 1:13
Glass	Imperfect knowledge	I Corinthians 13:12
	God's glory	2 Corinthians 3:18
	God's word	James 1:23, 25
	God's nature	Revelation 4:6
	New Jerusalem	Revelation 21:18, 21
Goat	Devils	2 Chronicles 11:15
	Wicked	Matthew 25:32-33
Grapes	Judgment	Revelation 14:18
Grass	Life's shortness	Psalms 90:5-6
	Prosperous wicked	Psalms 92:7
	God's grace	Psalms 72:6
Grasshopper	Inferiority	Numbers 13:33
	Insignificance	Isaiah 40:22
	Burden	Ecclesiastes 12:5
H		
Hail	Wonders	Job 38:22
	Glory	Psalms 18:12
	Chastening	Isaiah 28:2, 17-22
	Wrath	Revelation 8:7

Hair	Smallness	Judges 20:16
	Complete safety	1 Samuel 14:45
	Fright	Job 4:14-15
	Great numbers	Psalms 40:12
	Grief	Ezra 9:3
	Respect	Proverbs 16:31
	Attractiveness	Song of Solomon 5:2, 11
	Affliction	Isaiah 3:17, 24
	Entire destruction	Isaiah 7:8
	Decline and fall	Hosea 7:9
Hammer	God's word	Jeremiah 23:29
	Babylon	Jeremiah 50:23
Handkerchief	Healing	Acts 19:12
Harvest	Judgment	Jeremiah 51:33
	God's wrath	Revelation 14:15
	Gospel opportunities	Matthew 9:37-38
	World's end	Matthew 13:30, 39
	Measure of fruitfulness	2 Corinthians 9:6
Head	God	1 Corinthians 11:3
	Christ	Ephesians 1:22
	Husband	1 Corinthians 11:3, 7
	Protection	Psalms 140:7

Head Continued

	Judgment	Isaiah 15:2
	Confidence	Luke 21:28
	Pride	Psalms 83:2
	Exaltation	Psalms 27:6
	Joy and prosperity	Psalms 23:5
Heat, hot	God's wrath	Deuteronomy 9:19
	Man's anger	Deuteronomy 19:6
	Determination	Genesis 31:36
	Intensity	2 Samuel 11:15
	Zeal	Psalms 39:3
	Impatience	Ezekiel 3:14
	Persecution	Matthew 13:6, 21
	Heavy toil	Matthew 20:12
	Real faith	Revelation 3:15
Heavy	Fatigue	Matthew 26:43
	Burdens	2 Chronicles 10:11, 14
	Sins	Isaiah 24:20
	Sullenness	1 Kings 21:4
	Discouragement	Proverbs 31:6
	Unwillingness	Isaiah 59:1
	God's judgments	1 Samuel 5:6, 11

Hedge	God's protection	Job 1:10
	Afflictions	Job 19:8
	Slothfulness	Proverbs 15:19
	Removal of protection	Psalms 80:12
	Law	Isaiah 5:2
Heifer (young cow)	Improper advantage	Judges 14:18
	Contentment	Jeremiah 50:11
	Overindulging	Amos 4:1
	Obstinacy	Hosea 4:16
Herbs (leafy vegetables)	Resurrection	Isaiah 26:19
High	Rich	Psalms 49:2
	Pride	Psalms 101:5
	Superior standing	1 Chronicles 17:17
	God's mercy	Psalms 103:11
Highway	Holy way	Proverbs 16:17
	Gospel's call	Isaiah 40:3
	Way of salvation	Isaiah 35:8-10
	Two destinies	Matthew 7:13-14
	Christ	John 14:6
Honey	God's Word	Psalms 19:10
	God's blessings	Exodus 3:8, 17
	Wisdom	Proverbs 24:13-14

Honey Continued

	Pleasant words	Proverbs 16:24
	Prostitute's enticements	Proverbs 5:3
Hook	God's sovereignty	2 Kings 19:28
Horn	God's power	Habakkuk 3:4
	Christ's power	Revelation 5:6
	Power of the wicked	Psalms 22:21
	Power of the antichrist	Revelation 13:1
	Arrogance	1Kings 22:11
	Conquests	Deuteronomy 33:17
	Exaltation	1 Samuel 2:1, 10
	Degradation	Job 16:15
	Destruction	Jeremiah 48:25
	Salvation	Luke 1:69
Hornets (wasps)	God's agents	Exodus 23:28
Horse	Human trust	Hosea 14:3
	Obstinacy	Psalms 32:9
	God's protection	2 Kings 2:11
Hour	Gospel age	John 4:21
	Great tribulation	Revelation 3:10
	God's judgment	Revelation 14:7. 15
	Christ's return	Matthew 24:42, 44, 50

House	Grave	Job 30:23
	Body	2 Corinthians 5:1
	Believers	Galatians 6:10
	True church	Hebrews 10:21
	Earthly life	Psalms 119:54
	Heaven	John 14:2
	Security, insecurity	Matthew 7:24-27
	Division	Mark 3:25
I		
Increase	Messiah's kingdom	Isaiah 9:7
	Wisdom	Luke 2:52
	Faith	Luke 17:5
	Esteem	John 3:30
	God's Word	Acts 6:7
	Knowledge of God	Colossians 1:10
	Love	1 Thessalonians 4:9-10
Iron	Affliction	Deuteronomy 4:20
	Barrenness	Deuteronomy 28:23
	Authority	Psalms 2:9
	Stubbornness	Isaiah 48:4
	Slavery	Jeremiah 28:13-14
	Strength	Daniel 2:33-41
	Insensibility	1 Timothy 4:2

Irrigation	Spiritual life	Isaiah 43:19-20
		Isaiah 58:11
I		
Ivory	Luxury	Amos 3:15
	Wealth	Psalms 45:8
J		
Jaw	Power over the wicked	Job 29:17
		Proverbs 30:14
	God's supreme authority	Isaiah 30:28
	Human trial	Hosea 11:4
Jewels	Belonging to God	Matthew 13:45-46
Joy	Victory	1 Samuel 18:6
	Sinner's repentance	Luke 15:5, 10
	Forgiveness	Psalms 51:8, 12
	God's Word	Jeremiah 15:16
	Spiritual discovery	Matthew 13:44
	Good news	2 Chronicles 7:13
	Name written in heaven	Luke 10:17, 20
	True faith	1 Peter 1:8
K		
Key(s)	Means of victory	Matthew 16:19

Kiss	Complete submission to evil	Hosea13:2
	Complete submission to God	Psalms 2:12
	Reconciliation	Psalms 85:10
	Utmost affection	Song of Solomon 1:2
L		
Lady	Babylon/World	Isaiah 47:5-7
Lamb (young sheep)	God's people	Isaiah 5:17
	Weak believers	Isaiah 40:11
	God's ministers	Luke 10:3
	Messiah's reign	Isaiah 11:6
Lame, Lameness	Extreme weakness	2 Samuel 5:6, 8
	Inconsistently	Proverbs 26:7
	Weak believers	Jeremiah 31:8
	Transformation	Isaiah 35:6
Lamp	God	2 Samuel 22:29
	God's Word	Proverbs 6:23
		Psalms 119:105
	Christ	Daniel 10:6
		Revelation 1:14
Lap	Used to decide the outcome of the lot	Proverbs 16:33

Leap, Leaping	Great joy	2 Samuel 6:16
	Renewed life	Isaiah 35:6
	Victory in persecution	Luke 6:22-23
Left	Weakness	Ecclesiastes 10:2
	Shame	Matthew 25:33, 41
	Singleness of purpose	Matthew 6:3
	Riches	Proverbs 3:16
	Full armor	2 Corinthians 6:7
Legs	Man's weakness	Psalms 147:10
	Fragments left	Amos 3:12
	Christ's stability	Song of Solomon 5:15
	Fool's Inconsistency	Proverbs 26:7
Leopard	Man's incurableness	Jeremiah 13:23
	Transformation	Isaiah 11:6
	Antichrist	Revelation 13:2
Letters	One's writing	Galatians 6:11
	Learning	John 7:15
	Legalism	Romans 7:6
	Christians	2 Corinthians 3:1-2
Light	God's nature	1 John 1:5
	God's Word	Psalms 43:3
	God's wisdom	Daniel 2:22
	God's Guidance	Psalms 78:14

Light Continued

		Psalms 89:15
	Favor	Psalms 4:6
Lightning	Swiftness	Nahum 2:4
	Brightness	Matthew 28:3
	God's judgments	Revelation 11:19
	Christ's coming	Luke 17:24
	Satan's fall	Luke 10:18
Lily	Beauty	Song of Solomon 5:13
	Spiritual growth	Hosea 14:5
	Christ	Song of Solomon 2:1
Line	Rule of life	Isaiah 28:10, 13
	God's Providences	Psalms 16:6
	God's judgments	Isaiah 28:17
	Gospel	Romans 10:18
Lions	Tribe of Judah	Genesis 49:9
	Christ	Revelation 5:5
	Devil	I Peter 5:8
	Transformation	Isaiah 11:6-8
	Victory	Psalms 91:13
	Boldness	Proverbs 28:1
	Persecutors	Psalms 22:13
	Antichrist	Revelation 13:2

Liver	Extreme pain or death	Proverbs 7:23
	Emotions or suffering	Job 16:13
Locust	Weakness	Psalms 109:23-24
	Terrible onslaught	Isaiah 33:4
	Final plagues	Revelation 9:3, 7
Luxuries	Temptation	Joshua 7:20-21
	Physical weakness	Daniel 1:8, 10-16
	Moral decay	Nahum 3:7-19
	Spiritual decay	Revelation 3:14-17
M		
Marriage	God's union with Israel	Isaiah 54:5
	Christ's union with His church	Ephesians 5:23-32
Mask	Deception	Genesis 38:14
Meat	God's will	4:32, 34
	Christ	John 6:27, 55
	Strong doctrines	1 Corinthians 3:2
Merchandise	Wisdom's profit	Proverbs 3:13-14
	Gospel transformation	Isaiah 23:18
Melt, Melting	Complete destruction	Exodus 15:15
	Discouragement	Joshua 7:5

Melt, Melting Continued

	Defeatism	Joshua 5:1
	Destruction of the wicked	Psalms 68:2
	National discouragement	Isaiah 19:1
	God's presence	Micah 1:4
	Testings	Jeremiah 9:7
	Christ's pain on the Cross	Psalms 22:14
Milk	Abundance	Deuteronomy 32:14
	Elementary teaching	1 Corinthians 3:2
	Pure doctrine	1 Peter 2:2
Mire (deep mud)	Affliction	Job 30:19
	Eternal prosperity	Job 8:11
	Insecurity	Isaiah 57:20
	Subjection	2 Samuel 23:43
	Plentifulness	Zachariah 9:3
Moon	Eternity	Psalms 72:5, 7
	Universal praise	Isaiah 66:23
Moon Continued		
	God's faithfulness	Jeremiah 31:35-37
Morning	Man's unrighteousness	Hosea 6:4

Morning Continued

	Judgment	Zephaniah 3:5
	God's light	Amos 5:8
	Christ's return	Revelation 2:28
Moth	Inner corruption	Isaiah 50:9
	God's judgments	Hosea 5:12
	Man's insecurity	Job 4:19
Mother	Israel	Hosea 2:2, 5
	Judah	Ezekiel 19:2, 10
	Heavenly Jerusalem	Galatians 4:26
Mountain	God's protection	Isaiah 31:4
	Judgments	Jeremiah 13:16
	Gospel Age	Isaiah 27:13
	Messiah's advent	Isaiah 40:9
	Great joy	Isaiah 44:23
	Great difficulties	Matthew 21:21
	Pride of man	Luke 3:5
	Supposed faith	1 Corinthians 13:2
Mule	Stubbornness	Psalms 32:9

N

Nail	Words fixed in the memory	Ecclesiastes 12:11

Nail Continued

	Revived nation	Ezra 9:8
	Messiah's kingdom	Isaiah 22:23, 24
	Messiah' death	Isaiah 22:25
	Atonement for man	Colossians 2:14
Naked, nakedness	Barrenness of land	Genesis 42:9, 12
	Separation from God	Isaiah 20:3
	God's judgment	Ezekiel 16:39
	Spiritual need	Hosea 2:9
	Wickedness	Nahum 3:4-5
	Shame	Micah 1:11
	Needy	Matthew 25:36, 38
	God's knowledge	Hebrews 4:13
	Unpreparedness	Revelation 16:15
Neck	Servitude	Genesis 27:40
	Severe punishment	Isaiah 8:8
	Hardness of heart	Exodus 32:9
	Willingness to work	Nehemiah 3:5
	Deliverance	Isaiah 52:2
Needle	Something impossible	Matthew 19:24
Nest	False security	Numbers 24:21, 22
	Lord's protection	Matthew 8:20

Nest Continued

	Full maturity	Job 29:18
	Something out of place	Proverbs 27:8
	Helplessness	Isaiah 10:14
Net	Plots of evil men	Psalms 9:15
	Predatory men	Psalms 31:4
	God's chastisements	Job 19:6
	Enticements	Proverbs 29:5
	God's supreme plan	Ezekiel 12:13
		Ezekiel 17:20
Nettles (thorn bushes)	Desolation	Isaiah 34:13
	Retreat for cowards	Job 30:7
Noise	Strong opposition	Isaiah 31:4
	Worthlessness	Jeremiah 46:17
Noon	Blindness	Deuteronomy 28:29
	Cleansing	Job 11:17
	Transformation	Isaiah 58:10
Nose, nostrils	Man's life	Job 27:3
	God's power	Exodus 15:8
	Anger	Job 4:9
	Supreme control	2 Kings 19:28

Nose, Nostrils Continued

	Something very offensive	Isaiah 65:5
Nurse	Judgment	Lamentations 4:4
	Provision	Numbers 11:12
	Gentleness	1 Thessalonians 2:7

O

Oak	Strength	Amos 2:9
	Judgment	Isaiah 1:29-30
	Haughtiness	Isaiah 2:11, 13
Odors (sweet)	New life	Hosea 14:7
	Prayers	Revelation 5:8
	Christian service	Philippians 4:18
Offspring	True believer	Isaiah 22:24
	True church	Isaiah 65:23
Oil	Prosperity	Deuteronomy 32:13
	Joy and gladness	Isaiah 61:3
	Wastefulness	Proverbs 21:17
	Brotherly love	Psalms 133:2
	Real grace	Matthew 25:4
	Holy Spirit	1 John 2:20, 27
Olive Tree	Peace	Genesis 8:11
	Kingship	Judges 9:8, 9

Olive Tree Continued

	Israel	Jeremiah 11:16
	The righteous	Psalms 52:8
	Faithful remnant	Isaiah 17:6
	Gentile believers	Romans 11:17, 24
	True church	Romans 11:17, 24
Open	God's provision	Psalms 104:28
	God's bounty	Malachi 3:10
	Christ's blood	Zechariah 13:1
	Man's corruption	Romans 3:13
	Spiritual eyesight	Luke 24:31-32
	Opportunity	I Corinthians 16:9
	Ministry	Colossians 4:3
Order	God's covenant	2 Samuel 23:5
	Believer's life	Psalms 37:23
	Man's sins	Psalms 50:21
Ornaments	Wisdom's instruction	Proverbs 1:9
	Received reproof	Proverbs 25:12
	God's provisions	Ezekiel 16:7-14
	Turning from God	Jeremiah 4:30
	Good works	1 Timothy 2:9-10
Ostrich	Cruelty	Lamentations 4:3

Ostrich Continued

	Desolation	Job 30:29
Oven	Scarcity, famine	Leviticus 26:26
	Lust	Hosea 7:4, 6-7
	God's judgments	Psalms 21:9
	Effects of famine	Lamentations 5:10
Ox (adult bull)	Easy victory	Numbers 22:4
	Youthful rashness	Proverbs 7:22
	Sumptuous living	Proverbs 15:17
	Gospel broadcast	Isaiah 32:20
	Minister's support	1 Corinthians 9:9-10
	Believer's persecution	Jeremiah 11:19

P

Pain	Mental anguish	Psalms 48:6
	Impending trouble	Jeremiah 22:23
	Distressing news	Isaiah 21:2-3
Palace	Messiah's temple	Psalms 45:8, 15
	Divine workmanship	Psalms 144:12
	Eternal city	Jeremiah 30:18
	True church	1 Corinthians 3:9
Pale	Shame	Isaiah 29:22
	Death	Revelation 6:8

Palm Tree	Righteous	Psalms 92:12
	Beauty	Song of Solomon 7:7
	Idols	Jeremiah 10:5
	Victory	John 12:13
Pasture	Restoration and peace	Ezekiel 34:13-15
	Kingdom of God	Isaiah 49:9-10
	Gospel	Isaiah 30:23
Pearl	Spiritual truths	Matthew 7:6
	Kingdom of Heaven	Matthew 13:45-46
	Worldly adornment	Revelation 17:4
	Heaven's glories	Revelation 21:21
Perfume	Christ's glories	Psalms 45:8
	Righteousness	Song of Solomon 3:6
	Spiritual prostitution	Isaiah 57:9
Pierce, Piercing	God's destruction	Numbers 24:8
	Harsh words	Proverbs 12:18
	Conflict of soul	Job 30:16-17
	God's Word	Hebrews 4:12
	Coveted riches	I Timothy 6:10
Pillar	God's presence	Exodus 33:9-10
	Earth's supports	Job 9:6
	God's supremacy over nations	Isaiah 19:19

Pillar Continued

	Man's legs	Song of Solomon 5:5
	Important persons	Galatians 2:9
	Church	1 Timothy 3:15
	True believers	Revelation 3:12
	Angel's feet	Revelation 10:1
Pillar of Cloud & Fire	God's wonders	Joel 2:30
	Presence among believers	Matthew 18:20
Pipe, Piper (flute)	Joyful deliverance	Isaiah 30:29
	Mournful lamentation	Jeremiah 48:36
	Inconsistent reactions	Matthew 11:17
	Spiritual discernment	1 Corinthians 14:7
Pit (a Hole)	Grave	Psalms 30:9
	Captivity	Isaiah 51:14
	Ancestry	Isaiah 51:1-2
	Snare	Psalms 35:7
	Harlot	Proverbs 23:27
	Harlot's mouth	Proverbs 22:14
	Destruction	Psalms 55:23
	Self-destruction	Proverbs 28:10

Pit (a Hole) Continued

	Hell	Proverbs 28:1
	Devil's abode	Revelation 9:1-2, 11
Pitcher	Heart	Ecclesiastes 12:6
	Weakness	Lamentations 4:2
Plow, Plowing	Repentance	Jeremiah 4:3
	Peace	Isaiah 2:4
	Prosperity	Amos 9:13
	Affliction	Psalms 129:3
	Destruction	Jeremiah 26:18
	Persistent sin	Job 4:8
	Christian labor	1 Corinthians 9:10
	Information from a wife	Judges 14:18
	Constant decision	Luke 9:62
	Perverse action	Amos 6:12
Pond, Pool	Fishing	Song of Solomon 7:4
	Washing	1 Kings 22:38
	Water supply	2 Kings 20:20
	Irrigation	Ecclesiastes 2:6
	Healing	John 5:2-7
Posts (couriers)	Speed	Job 9:25
Pot	Sudden destruction	Psalms 58:9

Pot Continued

	Merciless punishment	Micah 3:2-3
	complete sanctification	Zechariah 14:20-21
Potter (maker of earthenware)	Sudden destruction	Psalms 2:9
	Complete destruction	Isaiah 30:14
	God's supremacy over men	Isaiah 64:8
Pour	Christ's death	Psalms 22:14
	Holy Spirit's coming	Joel 2:28-29
	Holy Spirit	Ezekiel 39:29
	God's wrath	2 Chronicles 34:21, 25
	Blessings	Malachi 3:10
	Supremacy	Job 10:9-10
	Prayer and Repentance	Lamentations 2:19
	Extreme emotions	1 Samuel 1:15
Presents (gifts)	Conceal a treacherous act	
Prisoners	Inhabitants of Hell	Isaiah 24:21-22
	Gentiles	Isaiah 42:6-7
	Those in spiritual darkness	Isaiah 49:9
		Zechariah 9:11-12
	Afflicted righteous	Psalms 69:33
		Psalms 79:11

Prisoners Continued

		Psalms 146:7-8
Purchase	God's gifts	Acts 8:20
	Church	Acts 20:28
	Office	1 Timothy 3:13
Purification (cleansing)	Christ's atonement	Malachi 3:3
	Regeneration	Acts 15:9
	Sanctification	James 4:8
	Obedience	1 Peter 1:22
Purple	Sign of riches	Luke 16:19
	Royalty	Judges 8:26

Q

Quiver (case for arrows)	Children	Psalms 127:5
	Messiah	Isaiah 49:2

R

Raiment (clothing)	Redemption	Isaiah 63:3
	Imputed righteousness	Zechariah 3:4
	Purity	Revelation 3:5, 18
	Honorable position	Psalms 45:14
Rain	God's Word	Isaiah 55:10-11
	Spiritual blessing	Psalms 72:6-7
	Righteousness	Hosea 10:12

Rain Continued

	Final judgment	Matthew 7:24-27
	Hell	Psalms 11:6
	Earth's ingathering	James 5:7
Rainbow	God's covenant	Genesis 9:16-17
Reaping	Harvest of souls	John 4:35-38
	Trust in God	Matthew 6:26
	Gospel age	Amos 9:13-15
	Injustice	Matthew 25:26
	Payment for services	1 Corinthians 9:11
	Blessings	2 Corinthians 9:6
	Reward for righteousness	Galatians 6:8-9
	Punishment for sin	Hosea 10:13
	World judgment	Revelation 14:14-16
	Final judgment	Matthew 13:30-43
Red Dragon	Satan	Revelation 12:3-17
Red Horse	War	Revelation 6:4
Reed (marshes)	Weakness	Isaiah 36:6
	Instability	Matthew 11:6
	God's measure	Ezekiel 40:3
Rejoicing	God's blessings	Exodus 18:9

Rejoicing Continued

	God's Word	Jeremiah 15:16
	Assurance	Luke 10:20
	Salvation	Luke 15:6-10
	Persecution	Acts 5:41
	Reunion of believers	Philippians 2:28
	Exaltation	James 1:9
	Christ's return	1 Peter 4:13
Repentance	Reformation of life	Matthew 3:8
	Restitution	Luke 19:19
	Godly sorrow	2 Corinthians 7:9-10
Rest	Physical relaxation	Genesis 18:4
	Sinful laziness	Matthew 26:45
	Sleeping	John 11:13
	Confidence	Habakkuk 3:16-19
	Completion of salvation	Hebrews 4:3, 8-11
Ring	Sign of authority	Genesis 41:42
	Social status	James 2:2
River	Prosperity of saints	Psalms 1:3
	Affliction	Psalms 124:4
	Christ	Isaiah 32:1-2

River Continued

	God's presence	Isaiah 33:21
	Peace	Isaiah 66:12
	Holy Spirit	John 7:38-39
Rob, robbery	Dishonest gains	Psalms 62:10
	Holding back from God	Malachi 3:8-9
	False teachers	John 10:1, 8
	Taking supplies	2 Corinthians 11:8
	Something seized	Philippians 2:6
Rock	Refuge	Isaiah 32:2
	Foundation of the Church	Matthew 16:18
	Source of blessings	1 Corinthians 10:4
	Stone of stumbling	Isaiah 8:14
	Foundation of faith	Matthew 7:24-25
Rod	Authority	Isaiah 14:5, 29
	Christ	Isaiah 11:1
	Christ's rule	Psalms 2:9
	The Gospel	Psalms 110:2
Roe, Roebuck (deer)	Timidity	Isaiah 13:14
	Swiftness	2 Samuel 2:18

Roe, Roebuck Continued

	Good wife	Proverbs 5:19
	Christ	Song of Solomon 2:9, 17
Room, make room	Part of one's life	1 Kings 8:20
	Favor	Proverbs 18:16
Root	Material foundation	Jeremiah 12:2
	Remnant	Judges 5:14
	National source	Romans 11:16-18
	Cause	Job 19:28
	Source of evil	1 Timothy 6:10
	Judgment & destruction	1 Kings 14:15
	Restoration	2 Kings 19:30
	Spiritual life	Hosea 14:5
Rot (Decay)	Wicked	Proverbs 10:7
	Foolish wife	Proverbs 12:4
Run, Running	Eagerness in evil	Proverbs 1:16
	Eagerness in good	Psalms 119:32
	Eagerness in the Gospel	Ezekiel 47:2
	Joy of salvation	Psalms 23:5
	Christian life	1 Corinthians 9:26

S

Sacrifices	Christ's sacrifice	1 Corinthians 5:7
	Prayer	Psalms 142:2
	Worship	1 Peter 2:5
	Righteousness	Psalms 51:19
Saliva	Short time	Job 7:19
Salt	God's eternal covenant	Numbers 18:19
	Barrenness, desolation	Deuteronomy 29:23
	Good influence	Matthew 5:13
	Grace in the heart	Mark 9:50
	Wise speech	Colossians 4:6
	Eternal destruction	Mark 9:49
	Reprobation	Ezekiel 47:9, 11
Sand	One's posterity	Genesis 22:17
	Weight	Job 6:3
	Large number	Joshua 11:4
	God's thoughts toward us	Psalms 139:17-18
Scepter	Authority	Esther 4:11
Sea	Extension of the Gospel	Isaiah 11:9
	Afflictions	Isaiah 43:2
	Righteousness	Isaiah 48:18

Sea Continued

	Multitude	Genesis 22:17
	False teachers	Jude 13
Seal	Married love	Song of Solomon 8:6
	Hidden things	Isaiah 29:11
	Acceptance of Christ	John 3:33
	Believer's security	2 Corinthians 1:22`
	Assurance	Ephesians 4:30
	God's ownership of His people	Revelation 7:3-8
Seat (place of authority)	God's throne	Job 23:3
	Association with evil	Psalms 1:1
	Satanic power	Revelation 13:2
Second, 2nd	Christ	1 Corinthians 15:47
	Finality	Titus 3:10
	New covenant	Hebrews 8:7
	Hell	Revelation 2:11
Seed, sowing of	God's Word	Matthew 3:13, 32
	Spiritual blessings	1 Corinthians 9:11
	Christ's death	John 12:24
	Christian's body	1 Corinthians 15:36-49
Sepulcher (place of burial)	Hypocrisy	Matthew 23:27

Serpents	Intoxication	Proverbs 23:31-32
	Wisdom	Matthew 10:16
	Malice	Psalms 58:4
	Unexpected evil	Ecclesiastes 10:8
	Enemies	Isaiah 14:29
	Christ	John 3:14-16
	Satan	Revelation 20:2
Servant	Slave	Genesis 9:25
	Social interior	Genesis 19:2
	Officers of court	1 Samuel 29:3
	Worshipper of God	1 Samuel 3:9
	Messenger of God	Joshua 1:2
	Messiah	Isaiah 42:1
	Follower of Christ	2 Timothy 2:24
	One enslaved by sin	John 8:34
Shadow	Protection	Psalms 91:1
	Brevity	Psalms 102:11
	Evening	Job 7:2
	Rest	Isaiah 32:2
	Change	James 1:17
	Death	Matthew 4:16
	Types	Colossians 2:17

Linda Sharon Sanders

Shadow Continued

	Time of Old Testament	Hebrews 10:1
Shake, shaking	Fear	Isaiah 14:16
	Second advent	Hebrews 12:26-27
	Rejection	Luke 9:5
		Acts 18:6
Sharp	Deceitfulness	Psalms 52:2
	Falsehood	Proverbs 25:18
	Contention	Acts 15:39
	Severe rebuke	2 Corinthians 13:10
	Christ's conquest	Revelation 14:14-18
Sheep	Innocent	2 Samuel 24:17
	Wicked	Psalms 49:14
	Backsliders	Jeremiah 50:6
	Lost sinners	Matthew 9:36
	Christians	John 10:1-16
	Christ	John 1:29
	Saved	Matthew 26:31-34
	Church	Acts 20:28
Sheepfold	God's care	Ezekiel 34:1-31
Shepherd	God	Psalms 78:52-53
	Christ	Hebrews 13:20

Shepherd Continued

	National leaders	Jeremiah 49:19
	Church leaders	1 Peter 5:2
Shield	God's protection	Psalms 33:20
	Favor	Psalms 5:12
	Salvation	Psalms 18:35
	Truth	Psalms 91:4
	Faith	Ephesians 6:16
	Rulers	Psalms 47:9
Shine, Shining	God's blessing	Numbers 6:25
	God's Word	2 Peter 1:19
	Gospel	2 Corinthians 4:4
	Believer's life	Matthew 5:16
	Regeneration	2 Corinthians 4:6
	Believer's glory	Daniel 12:3
		Matthew 13:43
Shipwreck	Denial of faith	1 Timothy 1:19
Shoe	Preparation for service	Ephesians 6:15
	Protection, provision	Deuteronomy 33:25
	Alertness	Isaiah 5:27
Short	God's Power	Isaiah 50:2
	God's Plan	Revelation 22:6
	God's punishment	Romans 16:20

Short Continued

	God's provision	Isaiah 59:1-2
	God's Providence	Matthew 24:22
Shoulder	Coast land	Isaiah 11:14
	Notable persons	Ezekiel 24:4-5
	Destruction	Ezekiel 29:7
	Servitude	Isaiah 10:27
	Rebellion	Zechariah 7:11
	Messianic authority	Isaiah 9:6
	Blessedness	Deuteronomy 33:12
Showers	God's Word	Deuteronomy 32:2
	God's wrath	Ezekiel 13:11, 13
	Messiah's arrival	Psalms 72:6
	Gospel	Ezekiel 34:25-26
	Remnant	Micah 5:7
Shut, shutting	Womb	1 Samuel 1:5-6
	God's mercies	Psalms 77:9
Silk	Diligence	Proverbs 31:22
	Luxury	Ezekiel 16:10, 13
	Excessive, unrestrained	Revelation 18:12
Silver	God's Word	Psalms 12:6
	God's people	Zechariah 13:9

Silver Continued

	Understanding	Proverbs 3:13-14
	Becoming worse	Isaiah 1:22
	Divine rejection	Jeremiah 6:30
Sing, Singing	Victory	Exodus 15:1. 21
	Noisy Celebrating	Exodus 32:18
	Imprisonment	Acts 16:25
	Joy	James 5;13
	Lord's supper	Matthew 26:30
Sit, Sitting	Christ's session	Hebrews 1:3
	Christ's rule	Matthew 19:28
	Judgment	Matthew 25:31
Sky	God's abode	Psalms 18:1
	Righteousness	Isaiah 45:8
	Ultimate judgment	Jeremiah 51:9
Sleep	Slumber	Proverbs 6:4, 10
	Loneliness, despair	Jeremiah 51:39, 57
	Unbelievers	1 Thessalonians 5:6-7
	Death	John 1111-14
	Spiritual indifference	Matthew 25:5
	Wicked life	Psalms 76:5-6
	Prophetic vision	Daniel 8:18
Sling	God's punishment	1 Samuel 25:29

Sling Continued

	Captivity	Jeremiah 10:18
	Uselessness	Proverbs 26:8
Smoke	God's anger	Deuteronomy 29:20
	Our life	Psalms 102:3
	Spiritual distress	Psalms 119:83
	Weak nations	Isaiah 7:4
	Something offensive	Isaiah 65:5
	Holy Spirit's arrival	Joel 2:29-30
	Christ's gentleness	Matthew 12:20
Snow	Disease of Leprosy	Exodus 4:6
	Converted sinner	Psalms 51:7
		Isaiah 1:18
	Messiah's glory	Mark 9:3
	Angel	Matthew 28:3
	Risen Christ	Revelation 1:14
Soldiers	Christians	2 Timothy 2:4
	Christian workers	Philippians 2:25
Songs	Gospel age	Isaiah 26:1-2
	Christ's arrival	Isaiah 42:10
Sow, Sowing	God's Word	Isaiah 55:10
	Reward	2 Corinthians 9:6, 10
	Gospel	Matthew 13:3-4, 37

Sow, Sowing Continued

	Spiritual gifts	Matthew 25:26
	Gospel messengers	John 4:36-37
	Resurrection	1 Corinthians 15:36-44
	Eternal life	Galatians 6:8
Spices	Presents	Genesis 43:11
	Commerce	Genesis 37:25
	Royal favor	1 Kings 10:2
	Wealth	2 Kings 20:13
Spider(s)	Insecurity	Isaiah 59:5
Spitting, Spittle	Contempt	Numbers 12:14
	Rejection	Matthew 26:67
	Uncleanness	Leviticus 15:8
Spot	Sin	Jude 23
	False teachers	2 Peter 2:13
Spotless	Perfect offering	Numbers 19:2
	Obedience	1 Timothy 6:14
	Christ's death	1 Peter 1:19
	Believer's perfection	2 Peter 3:14
	Glorified church	Ephesians 5:27
Springtime	Nature's rebirth	Song of Solomon 2:11-13
Spring up (rise)	Trouble	Job 5:6
	Truth	Psalms 85:11

Spring Up (Rise) Continued

	Wicked	Psalms 92:7
	Gospel	Isaiah 43:19
	Righteousness	Isaiah 45:8
	Light	Matthew 4:16
	New Life	John 4:14
	Bitterness	Hebrews 12:15
Sprinkle	Regeneration	Hebrews 10:22
	Purification	1 Peter 1:2
Stars	Christ's first arrival	Numbers 24:17
	Christ 2nd arrival	Revelation 22:16
	Angels	Revelation 1:16, 20
	Princes	Daniel 8:10
	Judgment	Ezekiel 32:7
	False security	Obadiah 4
	Glorified saints	Daniel 12:3
	Those that deny the faith	Jude 13
Stink, Stinkiness	Hostility	Genesis 34:30
	Hell	Isaiah 34:3-4
Stocks (punishment device used in jail)	Idols	Isaiah 44:19
	Instrument of torture	Acts 16:19, 24
	Race	Philippians 3:5

Stocks Continued

	Affliction	Job 33:11
Stones (rocks)	Immoral, damned person, reprobate	1 Samuel 25:27
	Contempt	2 Samuel 16:6; 13
	Christ rejected	Psalms 118:22
	Gift	Proverbs 17:8
	Desolation	Jeremiah 51:26
	Heart of Unbelievers	Ezekiel 11:9
	Christ arrival	Daniel 2:34-35
	Conscience	Habakkuk 2:11
	Insensibility	Zechariah 7:12
	Gentiles	Matthew 3:9
	Good works	1 Corinthians 3:12
	Christians	1 Peter 2:5
	Holy Spirit's witness	Revelation 2:17
Straw (hay)	Transformation	Isaiah 11:7
	Something worthless	Job 41:27-29
Stoning (as punishment for):	Sacrificing children	Leviticus 20:2-5
	Divination	Leviticus 20:27
	Blasphemy	Leviticus 24:15-23
	Denial of faith	Deuteronomy 13:1-10

Stoning (as punishment for)

	Idolatry	Deuteronomy 17:2-7
	Juvenile rebellion	Deuteronomy 21:18-21
	Adultery	Deuteronomy 22:23-24
Summer	God's covenant	Genesis 8:22
	Industry	Proverbs 10:5
	Opportunity	Jeremiah 8:20
Sun	God's presence	Psalms 84:11
	God's law	Psalms 19:4-7
	Future glory	Matthew 13:43
	Christ's glory	Matthew 17:2
Swallow	God's judgments	Psalms 21:9
	Conquest	Jeremiah 51:34, 44
	Contriving evil	Psalms 56:1-2
	Captivity	Hosea 8:7-8
	Sorrow	2 Corinthians 2:7
	Resurrection	Isaiah 25:8
Sweet	God's law	Psalms 19:10
	God's Word	Psalms 119:103
	Spiritual meditation	Psalms 104:34
	Fellowship	Psalms 55:14
	Pleasant words	Proverbs 16:24
	Sleep	Proverbs 3:24

Sweet Continued

	Christians	2 Corinthians 2:15
	Christian service	Ephesians 5:2
Swim, Swimming	Tears	Psalms 6:6
Swine	Abominable things	Isaiah 65:4
	False teachers	2 Peter 2:22
	Loose women	Proverbs 11:22
	Reprobate	Matthew 7:6
Sword	Divine retribution	Deuteronomy 32:41
	Divine victory	Joshua 5:13
	God's judgment	1 Chronicles 21:12
	A prostitute	Proverbs 5:3-4
	Anguish of soul	Luke 2:35
	Law Enforcement	Romans 13:4
	God's Word	Ephesians 6:17

T

Table	Human heart	Proverbs 3:3
	Christian's heart	2 Corinthians 3:3
	God's provision	Psalms 23:5
	Intimate fellowship	Luke 22:30
	Lord's Supper	1 Corinthians 10:21
Tapestry	Sexually immoral	Proverbs 17:6
	Diligence	Proverbs 31:22
Teeth	Destruction	Job 4:10

Teeth Continued

	Holding on to life	Job 13:14
	God's chastening	Job 16:9
	Escape	Job 19:20
	Judgment	Psalms 3:7
	Hatred	Psalms 35:16
	Oppression	Psalms 57:4
	Greediness	Daniel 7:5, 7, 19
	Starvation	Amos 4:6
	Hired prophets	Micah 3:5
	Remorse	Matthew 13:42, 50
Tempests (storms)	Destructiveness	Isaiah 28:2
	God's wrath	Isaiah 32:2
	God's chastening	Job 9:17
	Furious troubles	Psalms 55:8
	God's judgments	Psalms 83:15
	Hell's torments	Psalms 11:6
	Raging destructiveness	2 Peter 2:17
Tents	Shortness of life	Isaiah 38:12
		2 Corinthians 5:1
	Heaven	Isaiah 40:22
	Increase	Isaiah 54:2

Thirst	Salvation	Isaiah 55:1
	Righteousness	Matthew 5:6
	Holy Spirit	John 3:37-39
	Serving Christ	Matthew 25:35-42
Thorn	Unbelief	Isaiah 32:13-15
	Judgments	Hosea 2:6
	Indolence	Proverbs 24:30-31
	Pain	Proverbs 26:9
	False prophets	Matthew 7:15-16
	Agent of satan	2 Corinthians 12:7
	Barrenness	Matthew 13:7, 22
Throat	Gluttony	Proverbs 23:2
	Source of evil	Psalms 5:9
Thunder	God's power	Job 26:14
	Control	Psalms 104:7
	Majesty	Revelation 4:5
	Visitations of judgment	Revelation 11:19
Tin	Worsening of condition	Isaiah 1:25
Travail (labor pains)	Redemption	Micah 5:3
	New Birth	Galatians 4:19
Treasure	Wisdom	Proverbs 2:4
	People of God	Exodus 19:5

Treasure Continued

	Man's spiritual possibilities	Matthew 12:35
	New Life in Christ	2 Corinthians 4:6-7
	Future rewards	Matthew 6:19-20
Tree	Righteous	Psalms 1:1-3
	Believer's life	Proverbs 11:30
	Wisdom	Proverbs 3:18
	Basic character	Matthew 7:17-19
	prosperity	Isaiah 65:22
	Judgment	Luke 23:31
	Eternal life	Revelation 22:14
	Covenant	Romans 11:24
Trumpet	A new king	1 Kings 1:34-41
	Religious event	1 Chronicles 13:8
Veil	Gentile blindness	Isaiah 25:7
	Jewish blindness	2 Corinthians 3:14-16
Vessels	Mankind	Romans 9:21-23
	Chosen person	Acts 9:15
	Human weakness	2 Corinthians 4:7
	Believers	2 Timothy 2:20-21
	Person's body or wife	1 Thessalonians 4:4
Vine, Vineyard	Purifying afflictions	John 15:2
	Peacefulness	1 Kings 4:25

Vine, Vineyard Continued

	Worthlessness	John 15:2, 6
	Fruitful wife	Psalms 128:3
	God's Kingdom	Matthew 20:1-16
Virgin	Christians	Revelation 14:4
Vomit	False teaching	2 Peter 2:22
	Judgment	Jeremiah 48:25-26
	Riches	Job 20:15
Wages	Spiritual death	Romans 6:23
	Unrighteousness	2 Peter 2:15
Wall	Defense	1 Samuel 25:16
	Safe abode	Ezra 9:9
	Great difficulty	Psalms 18:29
	Peacefulness	Psalms 122:7
	Self-sufficiency	Proverbs 18:11
	Disorder	Proverbs 25:28
	Salvation	Isaiah 26:1
	God's Kingdom	Isaiah 56:5
	Heaven	Isaiah 60:18-21
	Spiritual leaders	Isaiah 62:6
	God's messengers	Jeremiah 1:18-19`
	Protection	Zechariah 2:5
	Hypocrisy	Acts 23:3

Wall Continued

	Ceremonial law	Ephesians 2:14
	New Jerusalem	Revelation 21:12-19
Wandering	Denial of the faith	Psalms 119:10
	Dissatisfaction	Proverbs 27:8
	Idolatry	Jeremiah 2:20
	Hopelessness	Jude 13
	Spiritual restlessness	Amos 4:8
Water	Instability	Genesis 49:4
	Cowardice	Joshua 7:5
	Spiritual growth	Psalms 1:3
	Peace	Psalms 23:2
	Afflictions	Isaiah 43:2
	Persecution	Psalms 124:4-5
	Adultery	Proverbs 9:17
	Universal Gospel	Isaiah 11:9
	Salvation	Isaiah 55:11
	Gospel age	Isaiah 41:17-20
	Holy Spirit	Ezekiel 47:1-12
	Eternal life	Revelation 22:17
	Christ	John 4:10-15
	New Birth	John 7:37-38
Wax	Persecution	Psalms 22:14

Wax Continued

	Wicked before God	Psalms 68:2
	Of the mountains	Psalms 97:5
Wells	One's wife	Proverbs 5:15
	Mouth of the righteous	Proverbs 10:11
	Wisdom	Proverbs 16:22
	Salvation	Isaiah 12:3
	Rich blessings	Jeremiah 2:13
	False teaching	2 Peter 2:17
	The Holy Spirit	John 4:10
Wheat	Spiritual blessings	Psalms 81:16
	God's Word	Jeremiah 23:28
	Christians	Matthew 3:12
	Christ's death	John 12:24
	Resurrection	1 Corinthians 15:37
Wheel	Future things	Ezekiel 1:15-28
	Punishment	Proverbs 20:26
	Cycle of nature	James 3:6
	God's supremacy	Ezekiel 10:9-19
Whirlwind	Sudden destruction	Proverbs 1:27
	Passing of the wicked	Jeremiah 30:23
	Suddenness	Isaiah 5:28

Whirlwind Continued

	God's anger	Jeremiah 23:19
	Destruction by war	Amos 1:14
	God's might	Nahum 1:3
Wilderness	Desolation	Jeremiah 22:6
Wind	Life's shortness	Job 7:7
	Empty speech	Job 8:2
	Empty boasting	Proverbs 25:14
	Vanity	Ecclesiastes 5:16
	Calamity	Isaiah 32:2
	God's chastisement	Hosea 13:15
	God's judgment	Jeremiah 22:22
	Scattering	Ezekiel 5:10
	Restoration	Ezekiel 37:9
	Ruin	Hosea 8:7
	Holy Spirit	Acts 2:2
	False teaching	Ephesians 4:14
Windows of Heaven	Judgment	Genesis 8:2
	Unbelief	2 Kings7:2, 19
	Blessings	Malachi 3:10
Wine	God's wrath	Psalms 75:8
	Wisdom's blessings	Proverbs 9:2, 5
	Gospel	Isaiah 55:1

Wine Continued

	Christ's blood	Matthew 26:27-29
	Abominations	Revelations 17:12
Winking the Eye	Conceit	Job 15:12-13
	Pride	Psalms 35:19
	Evil	Proverbs 6:12-13
	God's long-suffering	Acts 17:30
Wipe, Wiping	Deeds remembered	Nehemiah 13:14
	Tears removed	Revelation 7:17
Wolf	False teachers	Matthew 7:15
	Gospel transformation	Isaiah 11:6
Worm	Insignificance	Job 25:6
	Messiah	Psalms 22:6
Wound	Discouragement	Proverbs 18:14
	God's chastening	Jeremiah 30:14
	Gossip	Proverbs 18:8
	Drunkenness	Proverbs 23:29-30
	Adultery	Proverbs 6:32-33
	Sin	Isaiah 1:6
Write, Writing, Written	God's real people	Revelation 20:12, 15
	Indelible character	2 Corinthians 3:2-3
	Innate knowledge	Romans 2:15

Yield	Surrender	Romans 6:13, 16
	Spiritual fruit	Mark 4:8
	Consecration	Romans 6:13, 19
	Chastisement	Hebrews 12;11
Yoke	Oppression	Deuteronomy 28:48
	Heavy burdens	1 Kings 12:4-14
	Submission	Jeremiah 27:8
	Bondage to sin	Lamentations 1:14
	Discipleship	Matthew 11:29-30
	Legalism	Galatians 5:1
	Marriage	2 Corinthians 6:14
	Helpers	Philippians 4:3

APPENDIX TWO
Sample Dream Interpretations

The following passages contain dreams I have received over the years from people requesting a dream interpretation. I want to breakdown each dream and then give you a possible interpretation using the guidelines I have set forth in this book.

Dream 1

This morning I had a dream of a teenage boy that was in the hospital dying. He was supposed to be a friend. I didn't recognize him, but I was talking to him in the hospital room and I told him he was going to be with Jesus soon. The next part he was sitting in a chair beside me and said "my feet are turning black." I looked down and his toes were black. Then he got pale in the face. I looked in the hall and saw his mother and I went out to her. I told her she had better go in cause he was about to go. She went in screaming and others followed her and then I woke up.

Dream Elements

1. Teenage boy, dying
2. Hospital
3. Thought he was a friend, did not recognize him
4. Told him he was going to be with Jesus
5. He was sitting in a chair
6. said "his feet and toes were turning black."
7. Face became pale
8. Told his mother he was about to go
9. Mother was screaming when told he dying

Dream Analytics

I believe this teenage boy is a believer because the dreamer told him he was going to be with Jesus. He is her brother in Christ and perhaps this is why she did not personally know him, but felt he was her friend. The dreamer was beside him as he began to die (his face became pale, which is indicative of death and his feet and toes turned black). In our society, black is associated with death.

In researching a biblical concordance, I found a scripture in the Old Testament where feet were associated with the act of dying.

Genesis 49:33
And when Jacob had made an end of commanding his sons, he gathered up his feet into the bed, and yielded up the ghost, and was gathered unto his people.

I then referred to the dictionary to further clarify "feet". They support the whole body, and toes support the foot. The teenager's support seemed to be dying. Could this have indicated the spirit, which supports the body leaving the body?

Possible Dream Interpretation

I believe this dream indicates the dreamer will have the opportunity to minister Jesus' salvation in some kind of hospice situation and give comfort to those who are about to die and their families.

Dream 2

In my dream, there were three of us in a room. Me another woman and a man. They were dressed in blue and ready for church. I looked in another room and my husband was also dressed in blue. I said, "ok God, what do you want me to wear today?" He said, a blue dress! Then I woke up.

Dream Elements

1. There were three (3) people in a room, two women and a man.

2. They were dressed in blue, ready for church.

3. She looked into another room and her husband was dressed in blue.

4. The dreamer asks God what He would like her to wear.

5. God answers that He wanted her to wear a blue dress.

Dream Analytics

Three (3) is the number is a number of divine completeness. Perhaps these chosen people were now ready for God's plan. Blue as we have already determined, is a color representing a prophetic, spiritual element. Apparel or clothing is used to define the wearer, in this case, their spiritual character. The three people were dressed and ready for church. I believes indicates they were spiritually prepared for ministry. The dreamer looked into another room and saw her husband dressed in the same color. Houses are symbolic of our lives and rooms are sectors of those lives.

The dreamer asking God what He wants her to wear may point to some uncertainty about her spiritual gift, ministry or calling since this is what the blue represents.

Dream Possible Interpretation

I believe God is preparing the dreamer to minister prophetically. He is about to place her among other prophets He has chosen, along with her husband with the same gifting. Her inquiry shows her doubt about God using her in this ministry, but God is faithful and assures her of this call on her life.

Dream #3

I was getting ready to go to school or work, but I was trying to find a reason not to go. I didn't have on any socks and my husband said, "here some you left in the car." I said I don't want to wear those because they are dirty. I might have to go to gym class. He said no one is going to look at my socks. So I put them on and we were almost to the school when we saw a car lot. We stopped by to check them out. A guy came out to greet us and we told him we needed something bigger. All of the cars were used, but I found one I like. It was a black SUV Cadillac and had a GPS phone and DVD players. It was used and kind of worn, but I could settle for it.

We asked how can we get it? They said this is how it works. We give you the car but you have to pay for the car fully in 90 days. The car costs 22,000. I told them I want the car, but how are we going to pay for it in 90 days? I felt like I was trying to figure it out how, but I felt disappointed because it wasn't going to work.

Dream Elements

1. Preparing to go to school or work, hesitant.
2. Did not have on any socks.
3. Husband found dirty socks for her from the car.
4. Dreamer did not want to wear them because socks were dirty.
5. Dream feared someone might see the socks were dirty.
6. Husband convinced her to wear them.
7. Still on the way to school, stopped at car lot.
8. Told car salesman they needed a bigger car.

9. Cars were used, but dreamer found one she liked.

10. All of the cars had GPS and DVD devices.

11. Car cost 22,000 had to pay for it fully in 90 days.

12. The dreamer felt doubt about paying for it in the dream.

Dream Analytics

Preparing for work or school may indicate preparation for a lesson through a trial God is about to take the dreamer into. None of us like trials or tribulations and it makes sense the dreamer would feel hesitant or concerned.

Socks are a soft covering for feet. We use our feet when we tread a path. The socks may represent something that makes walking or treading a path easier, since they would cover bare feet. However, the ideal covering would be shoes. The dreamer will come to realize what this is. The dreamer's husband gave her a dirty pair of socks out of their car. This would indicate she was familiar with the foot covering and used it in her current life. She feared someone seeing her dirty or used socks which may mean she was not overt with her faith, but is a believer. Perhaps her socks or protection for her feet is prayer, a favorite scripture, etc.

Cars signify our life and the type of car defines our life status. The dreamer and her husband pass a car lot on her way to school. They look at a larger, black car with GPS and DVD communications.

Black is a color signifying trials, sorrow, calamity, and challenges. GPS is an acronym for Global Positioning System. A GPS is a system of satellites, computers and receivers. Its purpose is to determine location by latitude and longitude. A DVD is a type of compact disc able to store large amounts of data of audiovisual material.

In the dream, the car costs 22,000. This number equals a multiplication of twenty-two times one-thousand. The number twenty-two equates to light and one-thousand represents God's divine completeness and the Father's glory. Ninety (90) is nine multiplied times ten. Nine is fruit of the Spirit and divine completeness. Ten is the number of testimony, law and responsibility.

Possible Dream Interpretation

I believe this dream may be telling the dreamer she is about to go through a trial which may be financial in nature or another situation which could be trying. Her socks are a covering for the path she is about to go and this path, or the purchase of this car will enlarge her faith. In any case, her faith will be challenged.

Because of the communications equipment she will have access to within this car, she will not be at a loss of direction and will have access to visual aids (more dreams maybe) to direct her through it.

I believe twenty-two in her dream means she will receive much revelation and spiritual insight. The number of days in which the payment is due may indicate a certain season where the fruit of the Spirit can be birthed in her life. Trials are not easy, but the Bible says we should count it all joy when we encounter them because through God they can yield so much wisdom and increase our faith in Him.

Dream #4

Dreamer's husband was looking in the trunk of a car. The car automatically started by itself. He jumped in the car and couldn't stop it. The gears were locked. He ended up driving in the line of traffic. Then he woke up.

Dream Elements

1. Husband looking in trunk of car.
2. Car started automatically.
3. He jumped in the car, but could not stop it.
4. The gears were locked.
5. He drove in the line of traffic.

Dream Analytics

Cars represent one's life going forward, but he was looking in the trunk. The trunk of a car is located in the rear of the car, or in the back of his life going forward.

The gear that propels the car forward was locked in one position and could not be changed. The car starting by itself indicates that someone else initiated the power of the car to go forward.

The dreamer jumped the in car life moving forward and it

would not stop. Other cars or the traffic were going in the same direction. He was driving in the line of traffic.

Possible Dream Interpretation

I feel the Lord is saying to this man through his dream he is seeking things of the past, remembering perhaps what God did, things in his past life. God supernaturally begins to put him on a path or in circumstances that he can't change. The direction that he is about to take is God's sovereign will. Even though he tried to intervene, it will take place anyway. He had no control. God was taking him where he would not normally go.

Perhaps he would never go this direction by himself because he was uncomfortable and God made the decision for him. Maybe this dream is about a ministry calling or a change in his lifestyle. God has made it clear He is in control.

These four dreams are real dreams from four different dreamers. I have given examples from each of how a dream can be analyzed, dissected and examined. With prayer, you will come understand more and more the Dreams of the Lord.

Receive Jesus Christ as Your Savior

Romans 10:9-10

[9]That if thou shalt confess with thy mouth the Lord Jesus, and shalt believe in thine heart that God hath raised him from the dead, thou shalt be saved.

[10]For with the heart man believeth unto righteousness; and with the mouth confession is made unto salvation.

To invite Jesus Christ into your heart say this prayer:

Dear Jesus:

I confess to You I am a sinner. I ask You to forgive all my sins and cleanse me of all unrighteousness.

I ask You to come into my heart and become my Lord and Savior.

I believe You died on the Cross for my sins, but also so I can live in eternity with You.

With Your help and grace, I turn from my sin.

Write my name in Your Lamb's Book of Life and save me from the wrath to come.

Send the Holy Spirit to seal me and to let me know You are real.

I thank you for Your love and goodness toward me,

In the Name of Jesus.

ABOUT THE AUTHOR

Linda Sharon Sanders has been ordained in the ministry of the Gospel of Jesus Christ since 1998. God first pricked her heart to understand dreams and visions while attending a prophetic conference in 2008. Since then God has given her wisdom regarding the dreams and visions that each of us receives regularly as communication from God.

On her former radio broadcast, *The Dream Interpreter*, she regularly received the dreams of listeners and discussed their possible biblical meanings.

This book will give the dreamer insight about the Dream of the Lord, why God sends this dream, its purpose and how to interpret the message God is trying to communicate through the dream.

You will also learn about the biblical meaning of symbols, colors and numbers that can give great insight to what a dream may mean.

Made in the USA
Middletown, DE
17 June 2022

67313140R00109